Prestel

C000125603

LIECHTENSTEIN MUSEUM

The Princely Collections

Prestel
Munich · Berlin · London · New York

© Prestel Verlag, Munich · Berlin · London · New York, 2004

The pictures were kindly made available by the Princely Collections
at the LIECHTENSTEIN MUSEUM

Front cover: Peter Paul Rubens, *Double Portrait of Albert (1614–57) and
Nikolaus Rubens (1618–55), c. 1626/27* (cf. p. 101)
Back cover: Nicolas Pineau, Golden Carriage of Prince Joseph Wenzel von Liechten-
stein, 1738 (cf. p. 13)

Prestel Verlag
Königinstrasse 9, 80539 Munich
Tel. +49 (89) 38 17 09-0; Fax +49 (89) 38 17 09-35

Prestel Publishing Ltd.
4 Bloomsbury Place, London, WC1A 2QA
Tel. +44 (20) 7323-5004; Fax +44 (20) 7636-8004

Prestel Publishing
900 Broadway, Suite 603, NY 10003
Tel. +1 (212) 995-2720; Fax +1 (212) 995-2733

www.prestel.com

Prestel books are available worldwide. Please contact your nearest bookseller or write
to any of the above addresses for information concerning your local distributor.

The Library of Congress Cataloguing-in-Publication data is available; British Library
Cataloguing-in-Publication Data: a catalogue record for this book is available from
the British Library; Deutsche Bibliothek holds a record of this publication in the
Deutsche Nationalbibliografie; detailed bibliographical data can be found under:
http://dnb.ddb.de

Edited by Johann Kräftner

Texts by Johann Kräftner (History of the Princely Collections) and Isabel Kuhl
(Rooms IV–X; based on texts written by Andrea Stockhammer, in collaboration with
Stefan Körner)

Project co-ordinated by Victoria Salley
Copyedited by Michele Schons
Translated from the German by Paul Aston
Designed by WIEN NORD PILZ Werbeagentur, Vienna, and zwischenschritt, Munich
Typeset and produced by zwischenschritt, Munich
Lithography by Grasl Druck & Neue Medien, A-2540 Bad Vöslau, Austria
Printed and bound by Grasl Druck & Neue Medien, A-2540 Bad Vöslau, Austria

ISBN 3-7913-3140-X (English edition)
ISBN 3-7913-3139-6 (German edition)
ISBN 3-7913-3141-8 (Italian edition)

Printed in Austria on acid-free paper

CONTENTS

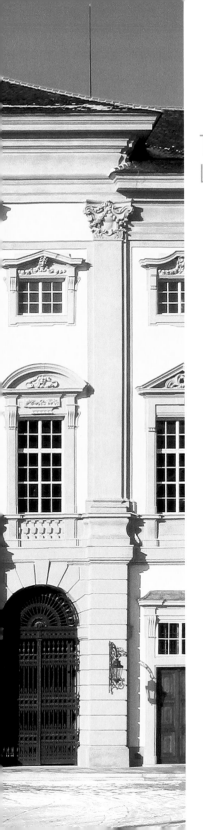

THE HOUSE OF
LIECHTENSTEIN

Santino Bussi 1664–1736
Detail of the decorative plasterwork
in the Sala Terrena, Liechtenstein
Garden Palace, post 1700

Joseph Kornhäusel 1782–1860
Gateway to the forecourt, Liechtenstein
Garden Palace at Rossau, 1814

Sala Terrena, Liechtenstein Garden
Palace

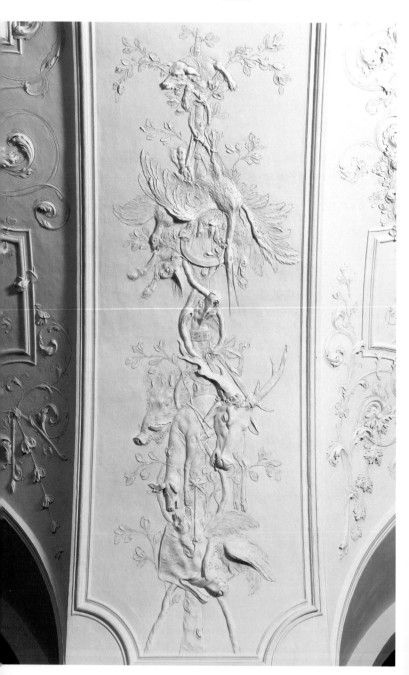

THE HISTORY OF THE PRINCELY COLLECTIONS

With the re-opening of the LIECHTEN-STEIN MUSEUM, the world's most important still extant privately owned art collection returns to its original historical location. Until 1938, it and other aristocratic collections in Vienna rivalled the old Imperial Collections that formed the basis of Austria's national museums today. All guides to Vienna from the 19th and early 20th centuries mention the importance of these aristocratic collections, which constituted one of the major attractions of Vienna both as a Habsburg imperial city and in its later guise as the capital of the young republic up until 1938.

The Princely Collections were among the most significant of these. Almost immediately after they were first shown shortly after 1700 in the Liechtenstein *Majoratspalais*, the head of the family's City Palace in Herrengasse,

Bernardo Bellotto 1721–80
Liechtenstein Garden Palace in Vienna Seen from the East, 1759/60
Oil on canvas, 100 ×160 cm

they were opened to the public, even if on a limited basis. Once they moved to the Garden Palace at Rossau to become the Liechtenstein Gallery, they formed the basis of one of the first publicly accessible museums in the city, with a huge range of paintings, sculptures, craft objects and furniture packed into it.

The works of art in the collection were always on the move, for they were distributed over not just a single gallery – though this was the core of the enterprise – but also over numerous residences and country houses across Austria, Bohemia and Moravia. Over the years, hundreds of objects were disposed of from time to time and whole collections of new items acquired. The collecting activities of the Liechtenstein family were dominated by the personal preferences of a number of individual princes. The result was that entire libraries and collections of prints and drawings might be assembled with remarkable speed – and later dispensed with equally quickly. Prince Johann II von Liechtenstein (1840–1929) was especially notable in giving away his possessions to half of Central Europe. The painting collection of the Vienna Museum, for example, owed its inception to a gift from him, whereas the painting gallery of the Academy of Arts in Vienna received its early Italian works from him and the Austrian Gallery in the Belvedere derived from the same source the most important works in its present collection of Biedermeier paintings, with major works by Ferdinand Georg Waldmüller and Friedrich von Amerling. Though the Kunsthistorisches Museum paid for the *Heroon of Gölbasy-Trysa* it acquired from him, Prince Johann II covered for the transport costs. Many major museums in Bohemia and Moravia were endowed by him with masterpieces still in their possession today.

Bernardo Bellotto 1721–80
Liechtenstein Garden Palace in Vienna Seen from its Belvedere, 1759/60
Oil on canvas, 100 × 159 cm

A passion for collecting obviously ran in the family, and is a tradition still alive today. However painful the losses may have been that the collections suffered as a result of events in the Second World War, in light of the dynasty's history they are perhaps events to which too much attention need not be paid, events that can be seen as a thing of the past. The House of Liechtenstein is currently still one of the few aristocratic families that has been able to continue actively collecting.

The first head of the family to be infected with the uncontrollable urge to collect was also the first prince in the family – Karl I (1569–1627). Spurred on by the collecting activities of Emperor Rudolf II, Karl started collecting and commissioning works of art. We know from correspondence between the two from 1597 that Karl already had a substantial collection of paintings and cabinet pieces in his Prague palace, and these stirred Rudolf's interest to such an extent that he wanted to exchange a number of pieces with Karl.

We have information from Valtice about a special Silver Vault: inventories tell us that in the *Guardaroba* Karl kept tapestries and carpets, costly furniture, gold and silver objects, vessels of precious stones and paintings, which formed the core of the Princely Collections. But Karl was active not only as a collector; he also commissioned major works of art for himself. For example, in 1607 Adriaen de Fries executed the lifesize bronze *Christ in Distress* for him, though we have no records of the *St Sebastian* Karl commissioned from the same artist.

His son Karl Eusebius von Liechtenstein (1611–84) systematically resumed what his father had begun and steadily developed the collection. His importance does not lie just in the fact that he collected, but also that he provided

West stairwell, Liechtenstein Garden Palace at Rossau

a sense of direction to the collection. His interests are evident in the treatises he wrote on architecture and the education of princes. Karl Eusebius steered clear of public office, and so had the time to indulge in his artistic and architectural passions. He initiated a whole range of building projects, and was the first prince of the House of Liechtenstein to employ architects, masons, plaster workers and painters in any number.

He initiated the building of a new parish church in Valtice, the foundation stone of which was laid in 1631. As an altarpiece for the high altar, in 1643 the prince bought Rubens's monumental *Ascension*, which is likewise now on view in the LIECHTENSTEIN MUSEUM. He was the first of his family to make systematic use of the art trade to buy paintings and sculptures. The beginning of the relationship with the Antwerp art dealer dynasty Forchoudt, who had a branch on Judenplatz in Vienna, dates back to this time. Whole collections were offered to him, from which he selected what was appropriate for his own gallery.

Along with his artistic interests, he also had a keen eye for horses, and the 'Schloss der Rosse', a great stable range built by Fischer von Erlach in Lednice, was the result of this second passion. He swapped the world-famous horses bred there with the second major collector of his day,

Archduke Leopold Wilhelm, in exchange – what else could we expect? – for pictures.

Karl Eusebius's son Prince Johann Adam Andreas I von Liechtenstein (1657–1712) picked up where his father had left off. A fortunate set of circumstances helped him. The Turks had just been thrust back for good from the gates of Vienna, and directly thereafter the prince began to acquire land on which to erect his summer palace. For the same reason he was able to

Giovanni Giuliani 1663–1744
Cartouche framing the Decius Mus paintings by Peter Paul Rubens, 1706

build numerous residences elsewhere too. Indeed, his architectural projects were so numerous that he became the greatest builder of the Baroque period in Central Europe. Decorating and furnishing them allowed him to pursue and develop his own ideas.

Among the land he bought was an excellent site in Herrengasse, where the splendid Liechtenstein City Palace was built shortly thereafter. Here he had space to realize his dream of displaying in worthy fashion the treasures in his possession. They included a number of major works that still account for the fame of the collection today. In 1693, for example, following protracted negotiations, he managed to acquire the Decius Mus painting cycle from Antwerp as the basis of an extensive Rubens collection. He commissioned no less an artist than Giovanni Giuliani to produce the frames and the cartouches of these works. The *Portrait of Clara Serena Rubens*, meanwhile, came to the Princely Collections from one of the most avid collectors of all, Archduke Leopold Wilhelm, whose own collection later formed the basis of the Kunsthistorisches Museum in Vienna.

The family's City Palace in Bankgasse must have been a veritable temple of the muses once it was completed. Along with the Imperial Collections, which were on show in the Stallburg at the time, it was undoubtedly one of the top attractions of Baroque Vienna in the early 18th century.

The varied interests of individual princes are reflected in the different strengths of the collections. Joseph Wenzel von Liechtenstein (1696–1772), for example, had become familiar with French art and come to like it during his stay in Paris (1737–41). He had used his time to commission works from a number of French artists. They include two fine portraits by Hyacinthe Rigaud and some pictures by Jean-Baptiste-Siméon Chardin, the latter being sold off during the period after the Second World War. The series of enamel paintings of the Trojan War by Pierre Courteys are among the most outstanding Limousin enamelwork of the 16th century. Finally, Joseph Wenzel also

Nicolas Pineau 1684–1754
The Golden Carriage of Prince Joseph Wenzel von Liechtenstein, 1738
in the Sala Terrena, Liechtenstein Garden Palace at Rossau

commissioned the famous Golden Carriage while in Paris. This is notable not
just for its artistic quality but also for its historic significance as the most
important surviving state coach of the French Rococo. Henceforth it will
occupy the centre of the Sala Terrena, or 'garden' room, in the LIECHTEN-
STEIN MUSEUM.

Thanks to the two pictures Joseph Wenzel commissioned from Bernardo Bellotto, we know what the garden and palace at Rossau looked like in 1759.
Joseph Wenzel also took a keen interest in books, and many of the manu-
scripts and other precious volumes in the library today were bought by him.
How wide-ranging Joseph Wenzel's interests were, particularly with regard to
sculpture (to which he, as head of the Austrian artillery and thus the imperial
foundries, felt a special obligation), is indicated by his purchase of the equestrian statue of Ferdinando I de' Medici by Giambologna. Commissions from
him likewise came the way of Austrian artists, including one for a pair of
near-lifesize lead-and-tin sculptures *Minerva* and *Apollo* by Gabriel Mollinarolo,

Library adapted from the Liechtenstein Chancellery in Herrengasse
by Joseph Hardtmuth, installed in its present location in the
Gentlemen's Apartments at the Liechtenstein Garden Palace at Rossau, 1912–14

which originally stood outside Joseph Wenzel's residence in Ebergassing and
were recently bought back for the Collections.

Under Prince Johann I (1760–1836), the Collections were moved in 1806 to
the Garden Palace at Rossau (1807–10), where there was substantially more
room for display than in the confined premises in Bankgasse. Even so, it
proved necessary to choose a form of display that left virtually no free space
between the paintings, as is clear from the hanging plans drawn up in 1815
by Joseph Bauer, which survive in their entirety. During his time as head of
the House of Liechtenstein the prince acquired 711 works, and by his death
the gallery contained 1,613 paintings.

When Prince Johann II (1840–1929) came into the succession, he completely
reorganized the gallery with the help of Jacob Falke – whom Alois II
(1796–1858) had called to Vienna as tutor to his children and as librarian –
and the assistance of Friedrich von Amerling. Anything that did not meet his
high standards he summarily removed and either dispatched to one of the
lesser residences or sold off without the slightest hesitation so that he could
buy something new instead. His own interests centred on 14th-, 15th- and
early 16th-century paintings, Gothic masters, Early Renaissance and early
Netherlandish art, as well as sculpture of the same periods. Other areas of
interest were Venetian masters of the 18th century and 19th-century painting.
He was guided in his collecting activities by Berlin art historian Wilhelm von
Bode, who drew up the first illustrated catalogue for the gallery, in 1896.

Andrea Pozzo 1642–1709
Ceiling fresco with the deeds of Hercules and his apotheosis, Hercules Hall,
Liechtenstein Garden Palace at Rossau, 1704–08

Hercules Hall, Liechtenstein Garden Palace at Rossau

Johann Michael Rottmayr 1654–1730
Mars and Venus
Detail of the ceiling fresco of The Military Spirit Being Admitted to Olympus,
east stairwell, Liechtenstein Garden Palace at Rossau, 1705–08

During the time of Prince Johann II's reign, the gallery took on the original and personal character that distinguished it from all other museums. The sober, clinical impression of a collection assembled on scientific criteria was deliberately avoided. The interior was enlivened and made less austere by the diversity of the art objects on show. The mixture of furniture, tapestries, craft objects, sculpture and paintings created the refined, warm atmosphere of a family house that set the Liechtenstein Gallery apart from other museums.

After a turbulent period during the Second World War, especially in the last
weeks of the war, when the Collections were transferred to Vaduz, there
followed a period of inevitable consolidation after huge losses of estates in
Bohemia and Moravia and the economic decline of the family's Austrian possessions. Since the complete reorganization of the business side into separ-
ate foundations by Prince Hans-Adam II von und zu Liechtenstein (b. 1945) in
the mid-1970s, the family has once again had a chance to pursue an active
collection policy, and particularly in recent times has acquired some excep-
tionally fine pieces. With his new acquisitions, Prince Hans-Adam II von und
zu Liechtenstein joins the ranks of his great forebears as a collector.
The major exhibition at the Metropolitan Museum of Art in New York in
1985/86 showed the world the importance of the Collections. The opening of
the LIECHTENSTEIN MUSEUM picks up the thread from there, continuing in
appropriate fashion the centuries of history of one of the most significant
private collections in the world open to the general public.

GALLERY IV

GOTHIC AND RENAISSANCE RELIGIOUS ART IN ITALY

During the 13th century, a variety of pictorial types emerged in Italy, ranging from altarpieces in churches to devotional images for private use. The period witnessed an evolution from polyptychs, divided into several fields by architectural features, to panel paintings conveying an impression of spatial depth. The leading role in this development was played by Tuscany, though in the Siena area Byzantine-style icon painting continued to enjoy great popularity, particularly as a source of inspiration for local painters. Compared with the variety of pictorial types elsewhere, the range of themes was limited, with madonnas predominating.

PASSION PAINTINGS

Christ as the Man of Sorrows was for many centuries a frequently depicted subject in pictures featuring scenes from Christ's Passion. In the Princely Collections, this type of Passion picture is represented by a painting by Naddo Ceccharelli. Active in the mid-14th century, the painter places the half-length figure of the dead Christ behind the sarcophagus covered with an embroidered cloth, suggesting pictorial depth despite the flat gilt background. Ceccharelli signed the painting on the sarcophagus, which is a measure of his self-esteem as an artist and his hope of benefiting from the salvation that the picture might deliver. In the ornate frame of the painting there are eight small round images of saints. Pas-

Naddo Ceccharelli active 2nd quarter of the 14th century
Christ as the Man of Sorrows, c. 1347
Oil on panel, 71 × 50 cm
IV.6

sion paintings of this kind were often used for private devotion, which gained in importance in tandem with an expansion of religious life beyond the narrow confines of church and monastery into ordinary everyday life. From the 13th century, this new kind of participation in religious life was substantially encouraged by friars of the mendicant orders. Terrible outbreaks of epidemics and famine did the rest to promote piety among the population. For the private devotions of theologically unschooled laymen, pictures were the most important means of conveying content and emotions of great import.

Giovanni Baronzio doc. 1345–62
*Adoration of the Magi, Crucifixion and
Seven Saints, c.* 1345
Oil on panel, 58 × 31 cm
IV.5

Giovanni Baronzio's *Adoration of the
Magi, Crucifixion and Seven Saints* is
in contrast an altarpiece – possibly
the centre panel of a winged altarpiece. In the middle of the painting is
the Crucifixion scene, with the three
magi above worshipping the new-
born Christ. The saints in the lower
third of the picture, especially St
Francis and St Clare, identifiable
from the robes of their respective
orders, can be linked with the Fran-
ciscans, suggesting that the client
who commissioned the picture had
something to do with the order. The
three fields of the mid-14th-century
panel are unified by a framed border.
The architectural character of the
subdivisions is emphasized by the
gable at the top, where Christ sits in
judgement.

MADONNAS

As the cult of the Virgin grew in the Middle Ages, visual representations of her
became increasingly important. Her role as an intermediary between man
and God made her the universal intercessor for believers. From the mid-13th
century, first in Tuscany, she is shown enthroned with the Christ Child. Often,
further panels with saints were arranged around this central image, resulting
in multipartite altarpieces. In the 15th century, the saints and angels in polyptychs of this kind were brought closer to the Mother-Child group, appearing
on the same panel and related to the main group compositionally. This type
of picture, with a group of figures gathered round the Virgin, is called a *sacra
conversazione* (literally, 'holy conversation').
The *Madonna Enthroned with Angels and Saints* was possibly the centre panel
of a winged altarpiece. Male and female saints and angels are grouped symmetrically around the Virgin's throne. The picture is ascribed to the Sienese
painter Gregorio di Cecco.
From the 14th century, the human and maternal aspects of Mary became
more prominent. The intimate relationship between Mother and Child featured

Gregorio di Cecco doc. 1389–1424
Madonna Enthroned with Angels
and Saints
Oil on panel, 45 × 26 cm
IV.3

Lorenzo Monaco doc. 1391–1423
Madonna with Child and Two Angels,
c. 1420
Oil on panel, 68 × 36 cm
IV.4

on many small-scale devotional pieces, such as the panel of the *Madonna with Child and Two Angels* by Florentine painter Lorenzo Monaco. The soft line carries echoes of the International Gothic Style, which enjoyed its heyday throughout Europe around 1400. The humility of the Virgin is likewise the subject of this picture. From the 15th century, she begins to be shown no longer seated on a throne but simply sitting on the ground – a pictorial type developed in Siena that is known as the *Madonna dell'Umiltà* (Madonna of Humility).

THE CONQUEST OF LANDSCAPE

In the Early Renaissance, the *Madonna dell'Umiltà* was no longer confined to interiors or set against a gilt ground, but was increasingly set in an expansive landscape. This often involved a new view of the Mother-Child relationship. Jesus was now more frequently depicted as a real child playing with his mother, or learning to read or make music. Sometimes they were joined by the young John the Baptist. Such apparently everyday scenes as Piero di Cosimo's *Madonna with Child and the Young St John* bear witness to the contemporary viewer's desire to get closer to the Virgin, who is most accessible

in her role as a mother. The Florentine painter took great care not only with
the details of the landscape and individual plants but also with the light effects.
A painter colleague of Piero's known as Franciabigio (his real name was
Francesco di Cristofano) shows a rather different encounter between the Holy
Family and John the Baptist, with the latter living in the wilderness. The scene
takes place on the Holy Family's return from Egypt, whither they had fled the
murderous Herod. In the background of the *Madonna with Child and the
Young St John* is the figure of Joseph outside the gates of a medieval city.
The artist foreshadows the death of Jesus by painting a dark fissure in the
ground beneath the feet of the Christ Child as an allusion to the rock tomb
where he was later buried. The Child Jesus holds a banner with the words
'ECCE AGN[US DEI]' (Behold the Lamb of God; St John 1,29), forming part
of the same forward reference.

Piero di Cosimo 1461/62–1521
Madonna with Child and the Young
St John, c. 1505/10
Oil on panel, 72 × 54 cm
IV.1

Francesco di Cristofano, called
Franciabigio 1482–1525
Madonna with Child and the Young
St John, c. 1518–24
Oil on panel, 121 × 90 cm
IV.9

Bernardino Luini's *Madonna with Child and the Young St John* presents a
northern Italian variant of the subject. He makes use of *sfumato*, a technique
in oils of which Leonardo da Vinci was the first great master. It enabled the
painter to achieve soft, flowing transitions between the various pictorial lev-
els. In contrast to many other paintings by Luini, the image was not subse-
quently transferred from its wooden ground to canvas, but survives in its
original condition.

Bernardino Luini *c.* 1480–1532
*Madonna with Child and the Young
St John, c.* 1515
Oil on panel, 83 × 66 cm
IV.8

The *Madonna dell'Umiltà* type was
also popular in the Veneto, as Moretto's (his real name was Alessandro
Bonvicino) *Madonna with Child and
the Young St John* demonstrates.
The Virgin is shown against the
backdrop of a city, sitting on a lawn
graced with numerous flowers. The
landscape with its architectural features is developed such that a sense
of depth is conveyed, and is no
longer there just to fill in the space
behind the figures. The harmonious
overall impression is aided by the
subtle coloration. In the sky are victor's laurels in an aureole. Belonging
to it is a panel held by the young St
John, the inscription of which antici-

Alessandro Bonvicino, called **Moretto** *c.* 1492/95–1554
Madonna with Child and the Young St John, c. 1550
Oil on panel, 38 × 51 cm
IV.15

Ferrara master
Christ in Repose,
c. 1480
Oil on panel,
54 × 35 cm
IV.2

pates Christ's victory over death: 'HIC ARMIS VICTOR DE ORBE TRIUMPHABIS' (With these weapons, Victorious One, you will conquer the Earth).

Landscape also found its way into other devotional subject matter. *A Christ in Repose* painted in Ferrara around 1480 is an example of a scene from the life of Christ intended for private devotion. The scourged Christ sits on a stone beneath vaulting, wearing the crown of thorns and a plain brown robe. The scene depicts the moment before Pilate presents him to the waiting rabble with the words: 'Behold the man!' ('Ecce Homo', St John 19, 4–5). The *Ecce Homo* was a popular devotional scene. The artistic achievement of the Renaissance is evident in this work not only in the introduction of the landscape. The painter also adheres closely to the rules of perspective, making all the lines converge in a single vanishing point, at the hands of Jesus. This strict use of central perspective enables him to create an impression of spatial depth.

Marco Palmezzano's *Christ as the Man of Sorrows* is likewise set against the background of a landscape. The Son of God shows us his wounds, but much of the horror of them is taken from them, and his immaculate divine beauty remains unimpaired. The sparing touches of vegetation and rocks directly

Marco Palmezzano 1459/63–1539
Christ as the Man of Sorrows
Oil on panel, 91 × 63 cm
IV.10

behind the figure of Christ, which abruptly become cloudy sky, are not suffi-
cient to convey a sense of spatial depth.

Likewise layered rather than spatial in effect is the landscape background in
Marco Basaiti's *Madonna with Child*. The Venetian painter shows the Christ
Child standing on a stone slab with his hand raised in a gesture of blessing.
The slab alludes to his future tomb. The figures fill the picture and, owing to
the contrast of dark and light, appear almost to emerge as three-dimensional
figures from the surface of the picture.

Marco Basaiti doc. 1496–1530
Madonna with Child, c. 1500
Oil on panel cradled, 64 × 51 cm
IV.7

A VARIETY OF PICTORIAL TYPES

In the High Renaissance, the horizontal format with one or more half-length figures enjoyed great popularity among religious images. The *Madonna with Child and St Anthony* painted by Moretto in the 1540s was presumably commissioned as a private devotional picture, as the small format suggests. A heavy curtain evokes the majestic motif of the baldachin familiar from pictures of the enthroned Madonna. Apart from this, the Virgin seems to be in an ordinary setting – a further effort to make her more familiar and accessible. In the 15th century, a pictorial type had developed in which an extreme close-up gave it the quality of an icon painting. Vincenzo Catena, who was active

Alessandro Bonvicino, called **Moretto**
c. 1492/95–1554
Madonna with Child and St Anthony,
1540/45
Oil on panel cradled, 46 × 58 cm
IV.17

Vincenzo Catena *c.* 1480–1531
Christ Bearing the Cross, c. 1520/30
Oil on panel cradled, 47 × 38 cm
IV.14

in Venice, used this technique in his *Christ Bearing the Cross.* The scene
from the Passion is pared down here to the half-length figure of Christ carrying the cross. Compositional cropping of this sort first became a feature of
devotional pictures the previous century. The composition's parallels underline the calm, contemplative character of the panel and Christ's expression
of intense concentration, while the simple setting lends the work the aura of
a bourgeois portrait, making it easier for the viewer to relate to.

In 15th-century Florence, the tondo became a popular picture format, and the
one here of the *Madonna with Child, the Young St John and Two Angels* was
painted by Sebastiano Mainardi around 1500. The painter depicts the figures
in a contemporary interior, with a view out on to the landscape through

Sebastiano Mainardi *c.* 1460–1513
*Madonna with Child, the Young
St John and Two Angels, c.* 1500
Oil on panel cradled, diameter 82 cm
IV.13

Perino del Vaga 1501–47
The Holy Family, c. 1540
Oil on panel, diameter 85 cm
IV.18

Giulio Romano (?) 1499–1546
St John the Baptist in the Wilderness
Oil on panel, 178 × 154 cm
IV.11

arched windows. The distant outline of a city with tall, slender towers echoes the architecture of San Gimignano, Mainardi's home town.

Another tondo, by the Florentine painter Perino del Vaga, shows *The Holy Family*. Painted around 1540, the brilliant colours and striking modelling of the figures recall the work of Perino's more famous contemporary Michelangelo. It was he who introduced the athletic nakedness of Classical deities into the religious art of his day. In the Renaissance, physical beauty was taken as a symbol of divine nature, and thus was also permitted in works intended for churches. *St John the Baptist in the Wilderness* is attributed to Michelangelo's contemporary Giulio Romano. The saint's slender, muscular body is scarcely covered by the leopard skin. He sits in heroic pose on a projecting ledge. Beside him, a spring wells up as a symbol of baptism and the purity of faith.

Bertoldo di Giovanni *c.* 1440–91
Shield Bearer, c. 1473
Bronze with remains of fire-gilding,
height 23 cm
IV.24

Andrea Mantegna (?) 1431–1506
Marsyas / St Sebastian
Bronze gilded, height 35 cm
IV.22

EARLY RENAISSANCE BRONZES

Among the earliest bronzes in the collection is a small *Shield Bearer*. It was
made by the Florentine sculptor Bertoldo di Giovanni, who worked at the
Medici court. The muscular, naked man bears a garland and belt of tendrils.
Dating from around 1473, the small bronze figure holds a shield and a mas-
sive cudgel. Bertoldo was one of the first artists to devote himself entirely to
bronze statuettes as an art form in its own right.

The bronze figure of *Marsyas / St Sebastian* is possibly by Andrea Mantegna,
who worked mainly in Mantua. He was an artist of many talents (a painter,

Jacopo Sansovino 1486–1570
St John the Baptist, c. 1540/50
Bronze, height 53 cm
IV.19

draughtsman, engraver and probably also a sculptor), but no sculptures have as yet been securely attributed to him. The figure of Marsyas comes from Greek mythology. After challenging Apollo to a musical duel and losing, the satyr was punished by being flayed alive. However, the figure of a naked man chained to a tree trunk could possibly also be St Sebastian, who suffered martyrdom at the hands of archers.

In the mid-16th century, the Venetian architect and sculptor Jacopo Sansovino created *St John the Baptist*, in which the saint is shown as a penitent in the desert. The slender body of John the Baptist, who leans against the stump of a tree, is covered merely by a fur. The sculpture conveys the saint's repentance of his sins in his gestures, posture and facial expression – the careworn furrows on his temple, his stooping upper body, his hand on his heart.

GALLERY V

LATE GOTHIC AND
RENAISSANCE PORTRAITURE

Barthélemy d'Eyck doc. 1440–70
Portrait of a Man, 1456
Oil on parchment mounted on panel,
51 × 42 cm
V.7

A large number of 15th- and 16th-century portraits in the Princely Collections bear witness to the lively contact between artists north and south of the Alps. Painters from the north travelled to Italy, and brought back home works of artists from the south while leaving an enduring impression of their own on Italian art. The influence of the northern naturalistic style of representation extended as far as southern France, as the *Portrait of a Man* dating from 1456 indicates. The sitter, a young man in a black coat, looks out at the viewer. He stands behind a parapet, on which the fingers of his left hand are resting. The accurate rendering of physiognomy – the painter skilfully captured the man's irregularly shaped eyes – was a feature of Netherlandish portrait painting. Because of this accuracy of detail and delicate modelling in light and shade, the portrait is attributed to Flemish artist Barthélemy d'Eyck, a member of the famous Bruges-based family of painters who worked for two decades in southern France as court painter to René I, Duke of Anjou.

The *Portrait of a Lady* is likewise an instructive picture as it bears witness to the exchange of artistic ideas between north and south. The portrait of the elegant young woman in a red dress wearing a string of fine pearls is attributed to Bernardino Zaganelli da Cotignola and probably dates from around 1500. The artist took special care with the naturalistic

Bernardino Zaganelli da Cotignola
1460 or 1470–*c*. 1510
Portrait of a Lady, c. 1500
Oil on panel, 33 × 25 cm
V.6

Michael Ostendorfer after 1490–1559
Self-portrait
Oil on panel, 41 × 31 cm
V.3

Raphael 1483–1520
Portrait of a Man, c. 1502/04
Oil on panel, 48 × 37 cm
V.2

rendering of the jewellery, which gleams in the light. The light facial tones of the sitter stand out to great effect against the dark background, her finely modelled features being thereby emphasized.

In southern Germany, too, artists were influenced by both Netherlandish naturalism and Italian Renaissance painting. The decline in the importance of religious subject matter in painting as a consequence of the Reformation enhanced the status of portraiture. Moreover the new view of mankind in the Renaissance gradually changed artists' perception of their own role in society, and they began to cast off the shackles of the guild system. As a widely travelled painter, Albrecht Dürer was a particular case in point, his self-portrait manifesting an enhanced self-assurance and new confidence in his own work.

This confidence is also eloquent in the *Self-portrait* of Michael Ostendorfer, a painter from Regensburg. Ostendorfer depicts himself in an exquisite brocaded coat with fur trimmings, but also with the attributes of his profession. The brush and palette are placed prominently in the picture. However, the clue to the occasion of the self-portrait is probably the carnation the young artist is holding. In Ostendorfer's day the flower was a symbol of engagements and marriages, and this explanation is borne out by an inscription added later on the reverse: 'Michael Ostendorfer, Self-portrait as a Bridegroom'.

Bernhard Strigel 1460–1528
Double-Portrait of Dr Georg Thannstetter and Martha Thannstetter,
née Werusin (also called Merusin), c. 1510/15
Oil on panel, 42 × 29/28 cm
V.4 and V.5

PORTRAITURE AND LANDSCAPE

In the Netherlands, portraits with a landscape background were very much in demand in the 15th century. They rapidly came into vogue throughout Europe. The *Portrait of a Man*, painted just after 1500, bears witness to the spread of this form of depiction to Italy. Behind the half-length figure of the youth, a view opens on to a broad river landscape, which frames the sitter's head. Because of the simple, harmonious composition and the limited but strong colours the work

has been attributed to the Renaissance painter Raphael.
For his double portrait of Dr Georg Thannstetter and his wife Martha Werusin, Bernhard Strigel opted for a length of red fabric as a background, which leaves only a narrow strip of landscape visible. Thannstetter was a physician, mathematician and cartographer as well as personal physician to Emperor

Jan van Scorel (?) 1495–1562
Portrait of a Man, c. 1520
Oil on panel, 47 × 41 cm
V.8

Lucas Cranach the Elder 1472–1553
*Portrait of Elector Friedrich III
the Wise of Saxony,* after 1532
Oil on panel, 80 × 49 cm
V.10

Maximilian I. To emphasize the breadth of his learning, he had himself painted in the typical scholar's pose of the day, a half-length portrait in three-quarters' profile. The double portrait by Maximilian's court painter was presumably done on the occasion of the couple's wedding in 1515. The uniformity of background is Strigel's way of indicating that the two pictures belong together. Martha Werusin (or Merusin) wears headgear of fine white cloth, but her black coat and the red curtain in the background show through. Cloth headpieces of this kind covering hair and neck were seemly clothing for married women, even in early medieval times.

One of the first Netherlandish painters to travel to Italy to study Renaissance art was Jan van Scorel. The *Portrait of a Man* attributed to him was possibly painted on his travels. The man's characterful face is unsparingly rendered, the painter scrupulously distinguishing the textures of garments, hair and beard. Whereas the relationship of the figure to the background landscape is more typical of northern portraits, the soft modelling in light and shade – and even the sitter's dress – are more characteristic of northern Italian painting.

Monogrammist AG active
c. 1540
*Portrait of a Youth before
a Wide Landscape,* 1540
Oil on panel, 59 × 51 cm
V.1

FRIDERICH · DER · DRIT · CHVRFVR
VND · HERTZOG · ZV · SACHSSE

The *Portrait of a Youth before a Wide Landscape* was clearly painted north of the Alps. With aristocratic self-assurance, the young man occupies the entire width of the picture, only his head being framed by a view of a river landscape. In the tree in the upper right-hand corner are the attributes of falconry, as an indication of the young nobleman's high social status. Perhaps this portrait was intended as a kind of advert. In view of the carnation in his right hand, it could be one of the pictures that marriageable young men sent to smooth the way for a marriage proposal.

Barthel Beham 1502–40
Portrait of Duke Ludwig X of Bavaria,
1531
Oil on panel, 69 × 59 cm
V.9

PORTRAITS OF RULERS

In the 16th century, ruler portraits became a well-defined genre of public statement at German princely courts. They were not just records of faces, but during the rulers' lifetimes also acted as their 'representatives'. The full- or three quarters' length figure was generally reserved for rulers.

One of the most sought-after portraitists of his day was Lucas Cranach the Elder, who painted the *Portrait of Elector Friedrich III the Wise of Saxony* in the Princely Collections. It is one of 60 elector portraits by the painter, which thus constituted one of the first major serial commissions in painting. Friedrich III had himself painted by Cranach as a scholar not a prince. As a patron of artists and scholars, including Martin Luther, he dispensed with the insignia of power in this painting. His burly figure and resolute chin and broad face contrast with the almost delicate hands, which hint at Friedrich's sensitivity and mental agility.

In 1531, Barthel Beham painted the Wittelsbach Duke Ludwig X of Bavaria wearing a fine black coat with a sumptuous fur collar. Beham was successor to Dürer as court painter to the duke, and within a few years had done a

Hans Mielich 1516–73
*Portrait of Ladislaus von Fraunberg,
Count of Haag,* 1557
Oil on canvas, 214 × 113 cm
V.13

whole series of Wittelsbach portraits. The *Portrait of Duke Ludwig X of Bavaria* is presumably the companion piece of the portrait of Ursula von Weich, now in Ottawa, since she was connected with the duke in a quasi-marital relationship. Beham exercised great care in accurately rendering the various textures of fur, beard and skin, and this lends the figure great vividness. Spatial depth is suggested by the three-dimensional rendering of the garment and the shadows cast by Ludwig on the greyish wall in the background. The duke's hand rests on the parapet, seeming to loom out of the picture plane and so forming a link with the viewer.

A showy, full-length ruler portrait is Hans Mielich's *Portrait of Ladislaus von Fraunberg, Count of Haag* of 1557, who was then ruler of the eastern Bavarian county. As he was the last of his line, the count's life was marred by fruitless attempts to secure the family succession, which the Duke of Bavaria tried to prevent by dubious means. The Munich-based painter records the self-assurance and intransigence of the count, portraying him in his splendid armour with his hand at the ready on his dagger. With an exotic leopard at his side, Ladislaus stands beside a window through which we can see the snow-covered castle of Haag. Above it are the count's arms. But symbols of mortality also feature – a skull and an hourglass to the right of the shield allude to the fleeting nature of all human pursuits.

Francesco di Cristofano,
called **Franciabigio** 1482–1525
Portrait of a Man, 1517
Oil on canvas, 55 × 40 cm
V.12

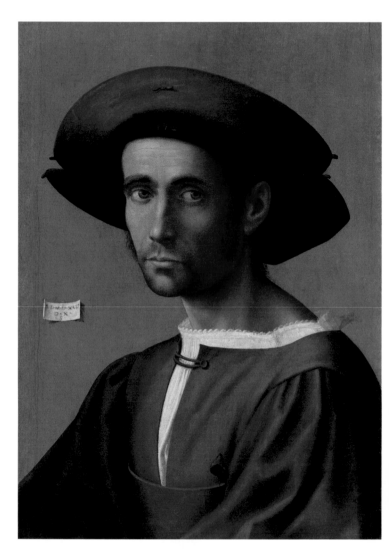

FLORENCE: FROM THE RENAISSANCE TO MANNERISM

An outstanding example of a Renaissance portrait is the *Portrait of a Man* by
Florentine painter Franciabigio, which is dated 1517 on the picture. The
painter opted for a cropped composition, recording the elegantly dressed
man against a green, otherwise indeterminate background, which directs all

Francesco Salviati 1510–63
Portrait of a Young Man, after 1548
Oil on panel, 89 × 69 cm
V.11

attention back to the shaded, melancholy features of the sitter. Franciabigio's interest in accurately depicting physiognomy and his efforts to produce psychological studies meant he was much in demand as a portraitist. The approach of Florentine artist Francesco Salviati in his *Portrait of a Young Man* was quite different. The soft facial features of the well-dressed youth shown in three-quarters' profile are calm, indeed emotionless, which was a highly regarded form of depiction in late-Renaissance portraiture. The character of the sitter was reflected in 'accessories' instead – in this case the fawn, which stands for shyness, gentleness and vulnerability. The sitter's rather artificial gesture and his slightly elongated figure are typical of Mannerism, as the last phase of the Renaissance is called (originally in the sense of 'stylish', but later meaning

Paris Bordone 1500–71
*Portrait of Nikolaus
Körbler*, 1532
Oil on canvas, 100 × 78 cm
V.16

Paris Bordone 1500–71
Portrait of a Bearded Man, 1533
Oil on canvas, 98 × 84 cm
V.15

Domenico Robusti, called **Tintoretto (?)**
1560–1635
Portrait of a Nobleman with his Son
Oil on canvas, 73 × 96 cm
V.14

'mannered'). Owing to his harmonious, yet richly contrasting palette Salviati was highly regarded as a painter, and even in his lifetime his reputation extended well beyond Italy.

THE COMPETITION: VENICE

Whereas Florentine artists were oriented towards clear contours and tangible plasticity, in Venice it was colour effects that attracted attention. Titian, more than any other artist, made 16th-century Venetian painting famous.

Successful Judenburg merchant Nikolaus Körbler commissioned a portrait of himself to celebrate his elevation to the nobility in 1532. Paris Bordone paints him in a large black outer garment with fur trimmings, in three-quarters' profile. The softly modelled face, calm gesture of the sitter and muted colours give the picture its harmonious effect. The *Portrait of Nikolaus Körbler* is

Andrea della Robbia 1435–1525
Relief Bust of a Young Man, c. 1470/80
Terracotta, coloured glazing,
diameter 70 cm
V.22

Pier Jacopo Alari-Bonacolsi,
called **Antico** *c.* 1460–1528
Bust of a Youth, c. 1520
Bronze, olive-brown patina covered
in black lacquer, height 57 cm
V.21

Bordone's earliest dated work. Less restrained is another work by the same artist, called variously *Portrait of a Bearded Man* or *Cavaliere Attaccabrighe (Sir Ruffian)*. A self-confident looking man stares out of the picture at us, boldly and provocatively grasping his dagger as a symbol of his alertness and readiness to fight. The dramatic lighting of the sitter in front of a dark round niche underline the slightly threatening features of his face.

In the *Portrait of a Nobleman with his Son*, attributed to Tintoretto, a vine reaches into the double portrait from the left, indicating the rural setting of a villa. The text visible in the boy's open book is a further reference to life in the country – it is Virgil's *Bucolica*, a pastoral poem that was often cited in support of the simple country life. In keeping with the Venetian painting tradition, here and there, for example in the child's waistcoat, the painter paid less attention to rendering the material accurately than to the effect of the colour.

SCULPTURE AND THE DECORATIVE ARTS OF THE RENAISSANCE

A different approach to representing the human face is revealed in two busts, by Andrea della Robbia and Antico (real name Pier Jacopo Alari-Bonacolsi). In their works, exact physiognomical renderings were less important than conveying a picture of ideal beauty.

The terracotta tondo with the *Relief Bust of a Young Man* dates from around 1470–80 and came from the studio of Florentine artist Andrea della Robbia. Given the even, idealized-looking facial features of the young man, this is probably less of

Giambologna 1529–1608 and
Antonio Susini doc. 1580–1624
Equestrian Statuette of Ferdinando I de' Medici, c. 1600
Bronze with traces of red-gold lacquer patina, height 64 cm
V.23

an actual portrait bust than a symbol of youth. The colourful glazed garland of flowers and fruit around the head could be a reference to this. The youth is leaning forwards out of the picture plane, which lends great vividness to the image.

Almost 50 years later, around 1520, the sculptor Antico created the *Bust of a Youth*. Here, too, the immaculately beautiful facial features bely the idea of pure portraiture. The softness of the locks and the fine, pensive features are reinforced by the gilding. The contrast with the unsparingly realistic portraits by northern artists in the same room could scarcely be greater.

An outstanding sculpture of quite a different kind is the *Equestrian Statuette of Ferdinando I de' Medici*, a bronze figure by the great Flemish-born Italian Giambologna and Antonio Susini dating from around 1600. The sculptors dispensed with any accurate representation of the ruler's face, simplifying the physiognomical features and concentrating on the work's overall air of grandeur, as was customary with equestrian statues. It was a portrait genre that expressed power and the high rank of the subject. While monumental equestrian statues would be erected in central squares of cities, small statuettes based on them were popular diplomatic presents.

A SHOWPIECE FROM THE IMPERIAL GEM-CUTTING WORKSHOP IN PRAGUE

In the 1620s, Prince Karl I von Liechtenstein commissioned the Italian artist Giuliano di Piero Pandolfini to make an ornate chest and tabletop decorated with Florentine mosaics. Mosaic was a classical technique for making pictures from cut stone, and came into fashion again at the end of the 16th

Giuliano di Piero Pandolfini doc. 1615–37
Pietradura chest, 1620/23
with the coat of arms of Prince Karl I von Liechtenstein
Hardstone inlays, garnet, gilt bronze, ebony, 56 × 88 × 49 cm
V.24

century. Pandolfini was the acknowledged master of it in the Castrucci workshop in Prague.

The Liechtenstein chest consists of a wooden core clad with stones. The latter are set in a gilt bronze frame. The front of the chest is divided into three sections and contains armorial devices and the client's monogram.

The same applies to the associated tabletop, the individual fields of which are subdivided by red-brown jasper. In the Baroque period, rare stones such as these were frequently compared with the prominent position of the prince in society, so that owning them was a ruler's prerogative. The magnificent tabletop by Pandolfini is decorated with landscapes, armorial bearings and other ornamentation.

Workshop of Castrucci
Pietra-dura tabletop,
1620/23
with the coat of arms of
Prince Karl I von Liechtenstein
Hardstone inlays, garnet,
gilt bronze, 93 × 89 cm
V.17

GALLERY VI

Theodoor Rombouts 1597–1637
The Denial of St Peter
Oil on canvas, 94 × 206 cm
VI.6

THE GREAT ITALIAN BAROQUE SCHOOLS

In the 16th and 17th centuries, Italian painting could be divided into two main styles. One went for an unsparing naturalistic rendering of reality, enhanced by dramatic lighting effects, while the other, trained on the art of Antiquity and the Renaissance painter Raphael, sought to idealize its subject matter.

THE NATURALISM OF THE CARAVAGGISTS

Favourite subjects of naturalistic painters were genre scenes depicting the everyday lives of ordinary people. Among these was the drinking session in the inn, such as Jean Valentin de Boulogne painted in the *Cheerful Company with Fortune-teller* in 1631. The fortune-teller is surrounded by musicians, quarrelling boon companions and other tavern folk. In works such as this, the painters also wanted to stir the viewer and gratify the senses. Boulogne exercised great care with the light effects in his pictures. He handled light and shadow with particular care so as to achieve striking contrasts. Such modelling of figures and objects by means of light is termed *chiaroscuro* (Ital. 'light-dark'). At the forefront of this technique was the painter Michelangelo Merisi, generally known as Caravaggio after his home town. In his paintings, he juxtaposed hard, clear light and deep shadow, which lent his works a dramatic effect. His subject matter – usually violent scenes from the Bible – was chosen so as to achieve an effect of directness through the realism of representation. Caravaggio's enthusiasm for spectacular lighting effects and realistic depiction attracted a large following among contemporaries and successors. Valentin de Boulogne became familiar with Caravaggio's work in Rome, and became the most important French Caravaggist in the early 17th century.

Caravaggism was equally popular in Dutch-speaking areas. Flemish painter Theodoor Rombouts studied the dramatic lighting in the Italian master's

Jean Valentin de Boulogne,
called **Moses Valentin** 1591–1632
Cheerful Company with Fortune-teller,
1631
Oil on canvas, 190 × 265 cm
VI.3

works and made use of it in his genre pictures. The protagonists of his works are mainly musicians, players and drinkers, which Rombouts re-used in ever-new compositions. Even in *The Denial of St Peter*, card-playing soldiers feature in the horizontal-format picture. Peter himself seems less a saint than an ordinary man. The painting depicts the moment at which the apostle denies for the first time that he is a follower of the captive Christ.

In Utrecht in the United Provinces a group of painters had discovered the work of Caravaggio for themselves in the early 17th century. Of the Utrecht Caravaggists, the best-known was Gerrit van Honthorst, whose particular forte was dramatic night scenes. *St Jerome* in the Princely Collections is by a follower of Honthorst. The body of the ageing saint is wasted from his perpetual penitential exercises, and the lighting from below emphasizes this. As a Father of the Church, translator of the Bible and writer Jerome was a popular subject in the Renaissance. South of the Alps, he was most commonly shown in the desert, while in the north he was usually found in his study.

Follower of Gerrit van Honthorst 1592–1656
St Jerome,
Canvas, 109 × 139 cm
VI.4

Occasionally both locations feature.
Johannes van Bronchorst, a late follower of Honthorst, painted *St
Bartholomew* in 1652. He shows the
apostle with a knife in his hand, as
an allusion to his subsequent martyrdom – he was later flayed alive. The
bare shoulder of the saint with light
falling on it from the left also foreshadows this event.

Johannes van Bronchorst 1627–56
St Bartholomew, 1652
Oil on canvas, 137 × 94 cm
VI.7

Girolamo Forabosco
1605–79
David with the Head of Goliath,
c. 1670
Oil on canvas,
121 × 97 cm
VI.5

Caravaggio's naturalism appealed to a group of painters in Venice as well, as Girolamo Forabosco's painting *David with the Head of Goliath* indicates. The slender shepherd boy David carries the head of the defeated giant to Jerusalem, and finds it tough going. Unlike most followers of Caravaggio, Forabosco does not use direct light sources or deep shadows but blends figures and their surroundings by soft modelling. The eschewal of sharp outlines in favour of painterly impressions and colour effects is characteristic of Venetian painting.

Paolo Pagani
1655–1716
St Jerome,
c. 1685/90
Oil on canvas,
118 × 149 cm
VI.2

Pietro Berettini, called
Pietro da Cortona
1597–1669
*The Punishment of
Hercules, c.* 1635
Oil on canvas,
300 × 200 cm
VI.1

Another *St Jerome* proves the popularity of *chiaroscuro* painting long after
the death of its inventor. Sometime between 1685 and 1690, Paolo Pagani
painted the saint as a hermit in the desert, whither he had retired to do peni-
tence. We are witnesses of a violent outburst of emotion. Jerome makes a
sweeping gesture with his right hand in order to beat his chest with a stone.
The illuminated body of the penitent looks as if compressed into the narrow
format of the picture, which underlines the force of his movement.

THE CLASSICAL STYLE

The principal representative of the non-naturalistic style was the Bolognese-
born painter Annibale Carracci. Active mainly in Rome and co-founder of an
academy, Carracci took as his models the beauty of nature, Classical sculptures and the clarity of Raphael's compositions.
This striving for ideal figures is also characteristic of the work of Pietro da
Cortona (real name Pietro Berettini), who devoted much time to studying
works of Classical Antiquity in Rome. *The Punishment of Hercules* painted in
the 1630s reveals the influence of Classical sculpture on the painter. The taut
pose of Hercules goes back to an influential, frequently studied Hellenistic
sculpture, the *Belvedere Torso* (now in the Vatican Museum). The monumental
painting shows an episode from Ovid in which Hercules is punished by Queen
Omphale for murdering Iphitus. She obliges him to wear women's clothes for

Francesco Solimena 1657–1747
Portrait of Prince Joseph Wenzel I von Liechtenstein, c. 1725
Oil on canvas, 126 × 101 cm
VI.12

Sebastiano Ricci 1659–1734
Battle of the Romans and the Sabines, c. 1700
Oil on canvas, 197 × 303 cm
VI.8

a year and be her servant. The picture records the humiliating moment when the hero is disarmed and fitted out with a dress and spinning distaff. Cortona's study of the torso sculpture is reflected in the painting, as is his interest in the *paragone*, the long-drawn out controversy in the 16th and 17th centuries as to which of the fine arts was superior. Was painting superior to sculpture, or was the opposite true? Painters weighed in with the virtues of naturalistic representation, while the sculptors drew attention to the multiple viewpoints and three-dimensionality of their works.

Around 1700, the successful itinerant artist Sebastiano Ricci made two pictorial contributions to the debate. His two large-format paintings *The Rape of the Sabine Women* and its companion piece, the *Battle of the Romans and the Sabines*, are a fair match for sculpture as far as multiple viewpoints are concerned. Ricci shows an episode from Roman history. As there was a shortage of women in the fledgling city of Rome, its very survival was under threat. The legendary co-founder and name-giver, Romulus, therefore had his men carry off women from the neigh-

Sebastiano Ricci 1659–1734
The Rape of the Sabine Women, c. 1700
Oil on canvas, 197 × 304 cm
VI.9

bouring tribe of Sabines. Ricci includes five symmetrically arranged pairs of figures in the foreground as studies of movement relating to the subject of abduction, thereby offering various viewpoints of the same subject, as in a sculpture.

The second picture records the continuation of the story, from the early days of Rome, and is set outside the city gates. To avenge the injustice perpetrated on them, the Sabines launched an attack on the Romans three years after the loss of their womenfolk. Unexpectedly, the women threw themselves between the combatants and separated them from each other. The sweeping gestures and whirling garments of the women underline their dynamic action. A further chapter of Italian Baroque painting was written in Naples. When the city was occupied by Austrian troops in 1707, art collectors in Central Europe suddenly became aware of the Baroque painters active there. Prince Joseph Wenzel I von Liechtenstein was particularly taken with the Neapolitan painter Francesco Solimena, to whom the *Portrait of Prince Joseph Wenzel I von Liechtenstein* is attributed. The picture depicts the pride and public ostentation of the successful prince, portrayed as both soldier and diplomat. In his armour, with his staff of command and sword, he stands in an aura of light in front of two monumental columns representing strength and power.

FORERUNNERS OF NEOCLASSICISM

Prince Joseph Wenzel von Liechtenstein also probably acquired two mythological paintings by the Roman artist Pompeo Girolamo Batoni. *Hercules at
the Crossroads* shows the youthful hero between two women. Voluptas (Sen-
suality) sits in the shape of Venus on the right, wooing him with roses, dice
and musical instruments and attempting to persuade him of the rightness
of a pleasure-filled life. Virtus (Virtue) appears here as Minerva, goddess of
counsel and wisdom. She holds out the prospect of toil and tribulation, as
demonstrated by the putti at her feet. But the goddess also draws his attention to the temple of fame at the end of the stony path, which Hercules ultimately finds more appealing. Batoni shows him still deliberating. Hercules
sits in the middle of the picture head on hand, weighing up the pros and cons
of both propositions. The clear composition, distinct outlines of the figures
and the even lighting of the scene make it easy to read. These were features
that anticipated Neoclassicism, the post-Baroque style that was oriented to
the clear, rational visual approach of Greek and Roman art.

Pompeo Girolamo Batoni 1708–87
Hercules at the Crossroads, 1748
Oil on canvas, 99 × 74 cm
VI.11

Pompeo Girolamo Batoni 1708–87
*Venus Presenting Aeneas with Armour
Forged by Vulcan*, 1748
Oil on canvas, 99 × 74 cm
VI.10

Very similar to *Hercules at the Crossroads* is its counterpart, *Venus Presenting Aeneas with Armour Forged by Vulcan*. According to Virgil's *Aeneid*, Venus
offered her son Aeneas the weapons forged by Vulcan so that he could hold
his own in the forthcoming battle. Batoni delighted in accurately painting the
details of the shiny weapons and armour, which are presented by two putti to
the right of the hovering Venus.

BAROQUE BRONZES IN THE PRINCELY COLLECTIONS

Antonio Susini (doc. 1580–1624) was Giambologna's (1529–1608) former
pupil and most important collaborator at the court of the Medici in Florence.
He specialized in bronze casting, particularly of Classical models and after
designs by Giambologna. At his death, he left Susini countless designs,
after which bronzes were cast in the latter's own workshop for many years.
Susini's *Rape of a Sabine Woman* is an example of a sculpture with numerous

Antonio Susini doc. 1580–1624
The Rape of a Sabine Woman, model
1581/82, after **Giambologna** 1529–1608
Bronze, red-gold lacquer, height 59 cm
VI.14

Antonio Susini doc. 1580–1624
*Deianeira Abducted by the Centaur
Nessus, c.* 1600
Bronze, height 43 cm
VI.18

viewpoints. You can walk round it without finding any neglected rear viewpoint. And as you walk, you follow the spiralling upwards movement of the group. This is called a *figura serpentinata*. Susini's design was inspired by Giambologna's marble group on the same subject, which had been exhibited in Florence in 1583. A male Sabine cowers on the ground, his wife attempting to wriggle out of the Roman's arms. Susini's bronze statue *Deianeira Abducted by the Centaur Nessus* depicting an episode from the Hercules myth was also executed to a design by Giambologna. According to the legend, the centaur Nessus helped travellers cross the River Evenus, but instead of setting down Deianeira on the opposite bank when she is entrusted to him, he attempts to rape her. The scene depicts the moment before Hercules shoots the centaur with an arrow, while the lovely Deianeira tries to escape Nessus's clutches.

Massimiliano Soldani Benzi 1656–1740
Medici Venus , c. 1699–1702
After an Antique model
Bronze, red-brown lacquer patina,
height 158 cm
VI.13

Like his father, Karl Eusebius, Prince
Johann Adam Andreas I von Liechtenstein had a penchant for bronze
statues. He maintained contact with
the celebrated Florentine bronze
caster Massimiliano Soldani Benzi,
who had been called in to assist with
the decoration of the prince's Garden
Palace at Rossau, and was commissioned to do a series of bronzes for
the gallery he planned in the City
Palace in Vienna as well.

Around 1700, the artist was working
on a bronze copy of the famous
Medici Venus. The marble original,
which derives its name from its later
owners, is an Antique copy of an
even earlier bronze. Its harmonic
proportions, balanced erect posture
and idealized features made the figure the epitome of Classical beauty
in the Renaissance. In the Baroque
period, the *Medici Venus* represented
for many artists a model of the
female nude.

The Judgement of Paris and *Diana and Callisto* are two other figural groups
by Soldani Benzi. The second group is shown the moment when Diana, the
goddess of hunting, discovers that one of her companions, who is bound to
chastity, is in fact pregnant. Callisto attempts to conceal the consequence of

Massimiliano Soldani Benzi 1656–1740
The Judgement of Paris, c. 1695/1700
Bronze, dark brown lacquer patina,
height 38 cm
VI. 26

**Massimiliano
Soldani Benzi**
1656–1740
Diana and Callisto,
c. 1695/1700
Bronze, dark brown
lacquer patina,
height 41 cm
VI.25

the encounter with Zeus, but she is unable to prevent her expulsion from the goddess's retinue. Diana is on the point of lifting her veil to pass judgement. This surprising moment of discovery was a popular subject in Baroque art. The busts of the *Anima Beata* and *Anima Dannata* are two casts in the Prince's collection by Soldani Benzi based on works by Gianlorenzo Bernini, one of the most versatile and influen-

tial artists of the Italian Baroque, who did the original studies of contrasting expression in 1619. The two bronze busts represent opposing states of mind – the redeemed and the damned. This interest in psychic extremes was also typical of Baroque artists. The *Anima Beata* looks up to heaven with wide eyes, her fine facial features framed by soft locks of hair. The male counterpart's hair stands practically on end. Cast out, the *Anima Dannata* stares at the ground with a distorted, aggressive mien.

Massimiliano Soldani Benzi 1656–1740
Bust of the Anima Beata, 1705–07
after **Gianlorenzo Bernini,** 1598–1680
Bronze, red-gold lacquer patina,
height 39 cm (without plinth)
VI.21

Filippo Parodi 1630–1702
Allegory of Vice, between 1684 and 1694
Marble, height 77 cm
VI.20

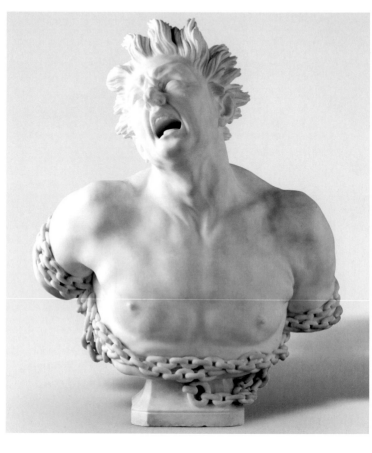

Filippo Parodi 1630–1702
Allegory of Virtue,
between 1684 and 1694
Marble, height 77 cm
VI.19

Console, Italy, *c.* 1730
Limewood, pine-wood, gilded, marbled, height 91
VI.15

Another pair of opposites in the prince's collection are two allegorical representations of Vice and Virtue, made by Filippo Parodi between 1684 and
1694. Bernini's *Bust of the Anima Dannata* was the inspiration for the *Allegory
of Vice*. It shows a man with chains around his arms and chest, suffering
great torment, but it also has a narrative context, since it depicts the giant
Tityus from Homer's *Odyssey* (11.576–81). The son of Zeus was condemned
to eternal torture for attempting to rape Leto. A pair of vultures tear at the
chained man's constantly replenished liver.
The pendant, the *Allegory of Virtue*, is adorned with several attributes –
a laurel wreath in the hair, the orb of the sun at the neckline and a small
spear under her right arm. She looks to her left, wearing a grave expression
on her face. Covering the transition between bust and plinth is a sumptuous
robe hanging in folds around the upper body, which conveys a slight sense
of torsion.

GALLERY VII

PETER PAUL RUBENS, ADRIAEN DE FRIES AND MASSIMILIANO SOLDANI BENZI

Peter Paul Rubens is considered the supreme master of Flemish Baroque. After spending eight years in Italy, he soon became the most sought-after painter in the southern Netherlands. Rubens was not just a successful artist, art collector and connoisseur of antiques but also the head of a large, productive studio that had clients throughout Europe. Despite his extensive business and family affairs, the highly educated, cosmopolitan artist also had time for tricky diplomatic missions he undertook on behalf of various European courts.

The Decius Mus cycle in the Princely Collections constitutes the earliest series of pictures Rubens ever painted. The monumental series was bought by Prince Johann Adam Andreas I von Liechtenstein, who immediately set the cycle of paintings up in a special room in the Liechtenstein City Palace in Vienna. From 1807 to 1938, they formed the pride of the picture gallery at the Garden Palace at Rossau, where they have now been returned. Rubens executed the large-format oil paintings as cartoons for tapestries that Genoese aristocrats had ordered from him. A contract survives between the artist and Brussels tapestry weavers Jan Raes and Frans Sweerts, under which Rubens was responsible for the cartoons and the final quality control of the tapestries. Doing such reversed-image designs in oils was by no means standard practice, but it made it easier for the weavers to recreate the painterly effects in their medium.

In view of the size of Rubens's studio, it is uncertain to what extent he personally contributed to many of the works produced there. That certainly applies to the 80 square metres of the Decius Mus canvases. The Prince purchased them in the belief that they were by Rubens's assistant Anthony van Dyck. However, the surviving 1616 contract makes it clear that the design (*invenzione*) of the pictures was by Rubens himself. At the time, the *invenzione* was considered the real creative phase. The Liechtenstein series is the first documented collaboration between the two painters, but attributing individual sections to Van Dyck is virtually impossible.

For commissions such as the Decius Mus series, the Rubens studio needed a whole repertory of figures and heads, for which numerous studies were done. One such, the *Head of a Bearded Old Man* of 1612, is also in the Princely Collections. Sketches like these aimed not to record the appearance of the sitter but, on the contrary, to achieve a type that could serve as a model for many figures.

Peter Paul Rubens 1577–1640
Decius Mus Relating his Dream, 1616/17
Oil on canvas, 294 × 278 cm
VII.1

DECIUS MUS RELATING HIS DREAM

The story of the heroic death of Roman consul Decius Mus derives from Livy.
One of the episodes in his multi-volume work *Ab urbe condita* (From the
Founding of the City of Rome) deals with the war between the Romans and
the inhabitants of Latium. The Latins challenged the ruling Romans to battle.
Two commanders, Decius Mus and Titus Manlius, were appointed, who both
had the same dream before the battle. It foretold that the victorious army
would be the one whose commander fell in battle. The Rubens series was the
first treatment of this episode in painting. The artist concentrates on the hero
of the story, with Titus Manlius appearing only in the last scene. In the first
picture of the series, Decius Mus is seen in imperious pose reporting the

Peter Paul Rubens 1577–1640
The Interpretation of the Victim, 1616/17
Oil on canvas, 294 × 412 cm
VII.6

dream of the past night to his assembled army. He stands on a platform in the left third of the picture, with his shield and helmet in front of him, and turns to face the soldiers standing below him. This raised position was also customary in the sculptures of commanders that Rubens had studied.

THE INTERPRETATION OF THE VICTIM

The next picture shows the soothsayer being consulted before the battle. A grey-haired priest (*haruspex*) performs the sacrificial ceremony outside the commander's tent, during which the entrails of two steers are read to determine the fate of the two army commanders. In the picture, a priest dressed in gold points at the liver of the bull sacrificed for Decius Mus. Part of it, in the shape of a head, is hacked off from the rest of the organ – and the fate of Decius was sealed. The commander recoils from the priest, his hands held protectively in front of him. The vivid scarlet of his toga visually links him with the sacrificial blood of the bull and the high priest's cloak.

Peter Paul Rubens 1577–1640
The Consecration of Decius Mus, 1616/17
Oil on canvas, 284 × 336 cm
VII.2

THE CONSECRATION OF DECIUS MUS

After the judgement is pronounced, the high priest blesses the doomed commander, who meanwhile stands with both feet on an arrow, as was the custom. Decius Mus is shown alone in the middle of the picture, his head bent
humbly to the ground and speaking the prayer of the dead. The light reinforces the solemn atmosphere of the scene. It brings out the shimmering
gold of the costly robe the priest wears and emphasizes his dramatic gesture. Also Decius's horse bows its head as soldiers bring it up, thus reiterating the commander's gesture of humility.

THE DISMISSAL OF THE LICTORS

Rubens depicts Decius Mus bidding farewell to his lictors in an extensive
landscape. With their heads bowed in sorrow, the officials take leave of their
commander, carrying with them the insignia of their offices, the *fasces.* In
parting from them, Decius also resigns his office as consul. Armed and
armoured, he is about to mount his horse. Beneath Decius's outstretched
arm, a gesture of farewell to the lictors, Rubens has included an edifice he
saw during his sojourn in Italy, the ruins of the Roman Temple of Minerva
Medica.

Peter Paul Rubens 1577–1640
The Dismissal of the Lictors, 1616/17
Oil on canvas, 286 × 343 cm
VII.5

Peter Paul Rubens 1577–1640
The Death of Decius Mus, 1616/17
Oil on canvas, 289 × 518 cm
VII.3

THE DEATH OF DECIUS MUS

The battle scene with the hero's self-sacrifice constitutes the culmination of the series. With the conflict raging all around him, Decius Mus is struck down by the lance of an enemy soldier. With his right hand he still grips the mane

Detail
VII.3

Peter Paul Rubens 1577–1640
The Obsequies of Decius Mus, 1616/17
Oil on canvas, 289 × 515 cm
VII.4

of his rearing horse, but his body is already slipping to the ground. The eyes of the dying man are directed towards the sky, the sombre grey of which is brightened by golden rays of light, symbolic of Decius Mus's elect role. The whole picture is filled with the violent, dynamic movements of attacking, falling and fleeing men, whom Rubens shows in diagonals in front and behind each other. The confusion of men and beasts can scarcely be disentangled, so intertwined are the figures.

THE OBSEQUIES OF DECIUS MUS

The last, horizontal-format picture in the series shows the funeral rites for the hero. Decius lies in his red toga on a gilt bier at the centre of the composition, with captive Latins cowering in front of it. In the right-hand corner, soldiers drag Latin women and children along by their clothes and hair. Behind the dead man is a pile of captured weapons, it being Roman custom to erect such a *tropæum*. A number of severed heads of the enemies are placed among them. For the first time, the other commander, Titus Manlius, appears. He stands to the left of the dead Decius and makes a sweeping gesture towards all the weapons, meanwhile watching the precious booty being brought in on his right. Behind Manlius, soldiers cut wood for the dead commander's cremation.

Peter Paul Rubens 1577–1640
The Assumption of the Virgin,
c. 1637
Oil on canvas, 501 × 351 cm
VII.8

THE ENTRE FENÊTRES

The original idea of the Decius Mus tapestries was to decorate a room in its entirety. To fill the smaller wall areas between the windows or beside doors, Rubens produced three designs called *entre fenêtres* (Fr. 'between the windows') on account of their function. One of the narrow formats shows a *tropæum* containing bits of armour, standards, weapons and captured treasures, as in the last picture of the series. The two other narrow pictures provide commentaries on the heroic deed of Decius Mus. One shows Virtus, the embodiment of military virtue, the other Victoria, the goddess of victory. The three *entre fenêtres* complete the Baroque picture cycle, the impressive overall effect of which is preserved thanks to close hanging. The almost life-size figures in the monumental picture format inexorably draw the viewer into the dramatic events. The strong colours and dynamic movements immerse viewers in the Baroque world, providing them with an experience that is unique in Vienna.

THE ASSUMPTION OF THE VIRGIN: A LATE WORK BY RUBENS

The *Assumption* in the Princely Collections is the last work by Rubens on this subject. It was a theme that over three decades he returned to time and again. The monumental, vertical-format painting dates from around 1637 and was probably commissioned by the Schotte brothers, who came from a prosperous Flemish family.

Anthony van Dyck 1599–1641
St Jerome, c. 1615/16
Oil on canvas, 158 × 131 cm
VII.9

Whereas the apostles in the lower half of the picture watch the ascension beside the empty tomb in astonishment, commenting on it with gestures, the Virgin rises on a cloud borne by angels. She kneels with outstretched arms, directing her gaze upwards. A halo surrounds her head, and numerous angels occupy the semi-circle around her. An unusual feature is the choice of white for the Virgin's robe in place of the customary blue. In this, Rubens reverts to the depiction of the transfiguration of Christ: like him, the Virgin is also dressed in white here. Overall the palette is light, which is characteristic of the late Rubens. Only in the final years of his work did he return to darker colours. Though he was now over 60, he seems to have painted the large-format *Assumption* mostly himself, as the bravura of the painting suggests. The painting passed into the possession of the Liechtensteins soon after it was painted, and from the late 18th century they exhibited it in their Viennese picture gallery.

ANTHONY VAN DYCK AS AN ASSISTANT IN THE RUBENS STUDIO

While working as an assistant in the Rubens studio from 1617 to 1620/21, Anthony van Dyck also executed works of his own. He was already making a name mainly as a portrait painter, but during this period also produced pictures with religious content, such as *St Jerome* of around 1615/16. In this large-scale painting, Van Dyck combines two different iconographic traditions associated with the saint: he shows him as a hermit in the desert, but also has him working on his translation of the Bible there, an activity generally located in a study. The combination of the hermit scenario popular in the south with the scholar generally favoured in the north indicates the lively cultural exchange across the Alps. The saint's ageing body is ema- ciated from his penitential exercises, and stands out against the red of the curtain. At his feet are not only books but also a lion, from whose paw the saint is alleged to have drawn a thorn. Thereafter the lion remained at his side.

Adriaen de Fries 1556–1626
Christ in Distress, 1607
Bronze with brown natural patina,
height 149 cm
VII.10

ADRIAEN DE FRIES AND MASSIMILIANO SOLDANI BENZI

Dutch sculptor Adriaen de Fries made two near-lifesize bronze figures at the behest of Prince Karl von Liechtenstein. The figure of *Christ in Distress* of 1607 is not based on any known written source. Sitting on a stone, Christ waits fearfully for Pilate's thugs. Fries skilfully balances the athletic body in its seated position, the face betraying his immanent suffering. 'EMPTI ESTIS PRETIO MAGNO' (Ye have been dearly bought), the words on the plinth, are from Paul's epistle to the Corinthians. They refer to Christ's role as

redeemer of mankind. Nearly ten years later the Dutchman did another bronze sculpture for the Prince, the two-metre tall *St Sebastian*. At orders of Emperor Diocletian, the saint suffered a martyr's death at the hands of bowmen. The frieze shows him before his martyrdom. Naked and helpless, he stands chained to a tree. The *contrapposto* of the figure is as complex as the

Adriaen de Fries 1556–1626
St Sebastian, 1613/15
Bronze with olive-brown natural patina,
height 200 cm
VII.11

seated posture of the *Christ in Distress*, and the surface treatment reveals the same artistic hand. The abstract effect of the surface, which is scarcely reminiscent of skin, is even more pronounced.

The small bronze cast *St Sebastian* was made in Italy in the early 17th century. It is the first of numerous replicas that enjoyed great popularity at the time. The slumped body of the saint was originally tied to a tree with ropes of silver, but these like his loin cloth have been lost.

David with the Head of Goliath was made by a pupil and colleague of Giambologna's, Giovanni Francesco Susini. Executed in the late 1620s, this piece may have been purchased by the well-educated and widely travelled Prince Karl Eusebuis von Liechtenstein as a 'souvenir' on his travels in Italy. Next to the oversized head of the giant with its veritable mane of hair the youth looks even more frail. He looks down at Goliath's head with a pensive expression, the huge sword of his opponent reiterating the giant's physical superiority.

Giovanni Francesco Susini
c. 1575–1653
Laocoön, 2nd quarter
of 17th century
After an Antique model
Bronze, dark red-gold lacquer
patina, 54 × 44 × 21 cm
VII.28

Laocoön is also the work of Susini. In 1506, a Classical marble group was discovered showing the Trojan priest Laocoön and his sons. Laocoön warned the Trojans against the famous gift of the Greeks, the 'Trojan horse', on account of which the goddess Athena punished him with death, arranging for him and his sons to be killed by a pair of serpents. Susini proved he could even improve on the dramatic pathos of the scene. His bronze cast of the world-famous work is reckoned the finest copy since Antiquity.

In 1695, Prince Johann Adam Andreas I von Liechtenstein commissioned the Italian sculptor Massimiliano Soldani Benzi to make nine bronze casts from Classical busts, including those of Emperor Hadrian and other famous Roman men and women. The same year the prince ordered a bronze relief from him. The *Bacchanalia*, the Bacchic rites of the god of wine, takes place amid lush vegetation. Wine is already at work. The festive company of all kinds of fabulous creatures is very merry indeed, with some of the individual figures falling over each other. Soldani Benzi created this masterly composition by making

**Massimiliano
Soldani Benzi**
1656–1740
Bacchanalia,
1695–97
Bronze with red-
gold lacquer pat-
ina, 56 × 78 cm
VII.24

Massimiliano Soldani Benzi 1656–1740
Christ on the Mount of Olives, c. 1722
Bronze with golden-brown lacquer
patina, 65 × 45 cm
VII.35

the foreground figures appear three-dimensional and the background architecture nearly flat, thus achieving an almost painterly effect.

Another relief by the artist, dating from around 1722, is *Christ on the Mount of Olives*, which looks almost like a devotional image. It shows Christ praying in a garden. Keeping watch the night before his crucifixion, he faints, but is supported by two angels. A diagonal line dominates the representation and heightens the dynamism of the scene.

The figural group in *The Triumph of Virtue over Vice* goes back to a marble work by Giambologna exhibited in Florence called *Florence Triumphs over Pisa*, one of the best-known sculptures in the city. These and other pieces were copied by Soldani Benzi and offered to Prince Johann Adam for purchase. Soldani Benzi's allegory of Virtue (Florence) conquers Vice (Pisa), which is shown as a man crouching on the ground. The immense physical effort in the preceding battle can be read on Virtue's face.

Massimiliano Soldani Benzi 1656–1740
The Triumph of Virtue over Vice,
c. 1701–06
after **Giambologna** 1529–1608
Bronze, dark brown lacquer patina,
height 31 cm
VII.34

GALLERY VIII

THE EARLY WORK OF PETER PAUL RUBENS

The Princely Collections have over 30 works by Flemish artist Peter Paul Rubens. Particularly the early works are well represented, which clearly show the influence of his long sojourn in Italy at the beginning of the 17th century. In the initial years of his career, Rubens did many pictures featuring less familiar subjects from mythology and ancient history.

MYTHOLOGICAL SUBJECTS

In Italy Rubens studied the works of Italian Renaissance painters and their followers. Amongst these, there were many examples of *Venus in front of the Mirror*, and yet his *invenzione* of around 1613/14 is all his own. He presents the goddess of beauty in a rear view, looking in a mirror held by her son, the love god Cupid. The viewer sees the face of Venus in the framed mirror, and in approaching her from the back seems to surprise her at her toilet. The fair skin, shiny hair and precious accessories of the naked goddess are painted by Rubens with a great love of detail.

Peter Paul Rubens 1577–1640
Venus in Front of the Mirror,
c. 1613/14
Oil on panel,
123 × 98 cm
VIII.1

Peter Paul Rubens 1577–1640
Maid with Fruit Basket, c. 1615
Oil on canvas, 113 × 71 cm
Schönborn-Buchheim
Collection
VIII.5

No less splendid in coloration is the small painting of the *Maid with Fruit Basket*. The satyr, a hybrid creature between man and beast from the retinue of the god Dionysius, offers the viewer a luscious basket of fruit. The flushed cheeks and broad grin testify to an immoderate consumption of wine – just as the tendril held by the girl beside him alludes to the god of wine. *Bacchus*, as the god of intoxication and pleasure is called in Latin, stands close to both, as a bronze. In Italy Rubens also studied Roman art. His extensive knowledge of

Massimiliano Soldani Benzi 1656–1740
Bacchus, 1699–1701
after **Michelangelo Buonarroti**
1475–1564
Bronze with red-brown lacquer patina,
height 198 cm
VIII.8

Peter Paul Rubens 1577–1640
The Discovery of the Infant Erichthonius,
c. 1616
Oil on canvas, 218 × 317 cm
VIII.4

Classical authors prompted him to explore rare subjects. In 1616, for example, he painted *The Discovery of the Infant Erichthonius*, from a story by Ovid. Three women, whose naked bodies are scarcely concealed by their skilfully placed drapery, have gathered round a basket containing a small boy. The serpentine feet of the baby are a legacy of his mother, the earth goddess Gæa. The fountain figure of Diana of Ephesus, a symbol of fertility and physical drives, alludes to the cruel pre-history of the conception of the boy. Vulcan attempted to rape the virginal Minerva, and only because she succeeded in escaping did his seed fall to the ground and impregnate Gæa. The figure seen from the rear at the right is an 'old acquaintance', bearing features of the figure in *Venus in Front of the Mirror*.

In the same year, Rubens took up another Classical myth. The large-scale painting of *Mars and Rhea Silvia* was preceded by an oil sketch that is likewise in the Princely Collections in Vaduz. Rhea Silvia was a priestess of Vesta, goddess of the hearth and families, whose shrine (seen on the extreme right) protected her. As a vestal virgin, Rhea Silvia had praised chastity, but the god of war, Mars, violated her and spawned Romulus and Remus, the legendary founders of Rome. Cupid functions in Rubens's work as a matchmaker between the two figures.

Peter Paul Rubens 1577–1640
Christ Triumphant over Sin and Death,
between 1615 and 1622
Oil on canvas, 182 × 230 cm
VIII.7

Peter Paul Rubens 1577–1640
The Lamentation, c. 1613/14
Oil on canvas, 151 × 204 cm
VIII.6

BIBLICAL STORIES

Rubens made frequent use of diagonals in his compositions, as in the *Lamentation* of around 1614. The grey, wan corpse of Christ just taken down from the cross forms a diagonal line. The viewer is close to the dead man, in fact almost opposite him. The Virgin closes her son's eyes and removes a thorn from his forehead, while St John supports her by the arm. St Joseph of

Peter Paul Rubens 1577–1640
Mars and Rhea Silvia, c. 1616/17
Oil on canvas, 208 × 272 cm
VIII.3

Arimathea catches hold of the slumping upper body of the corpse, while the women around Mary Magdalene lament the dead man.
Another early work is the painting *Christ Triumphant over Sin and Death*. The picture shows the risen Christ sitting on the open sarcophagus like a throne. In his right hand, he holds a white flag with a red cross as a symbol of resurrection. Angels hold a laurel wreath and palm branch as symbols of Jesus' victory over his martyrdom. On the right-hand edge of the picture, flames from hell dart forth and tell of the punishment for death and sin, represented by the skeleton and snake at Christ's feet.

BAROQUE BRONZES

Prince Karl Eusebius von Liechtenstein was not only an enthusiastic collector of Renaissance sculpture but also commissioned contemporary artists to execute works for his collection. At the end of the 1630s, he ordered two bronzes, *Apollo and Cupid* and *Mercury*, from Flemish sculptor François Duquesnoy. The former shows Apollo, the god of song and string players and leader of the muses, introducing Cupid to the art of bowmanship. Unfortunately Apollo's bow, whose taut string is held by the youthful god with his right hand, has been lost. There was originally a Cupid for the counterpart

François Duquesnoy 1597–1643
Apollo and Cupid, c. 1635/40
Bronze with light brown lacquer patina,
66 × 27 cm
VIII.13

François Duquesnoy 1597–1643
Mercury, c. 1630/40
Bronze with light brown lacquer patina,
63 × 28 cm
VIII.14

figure of Mercury as well. Mercury, as the god of commerce, also served as a messenger of the gods, so he is often given the attribute of winged feet. The Cupid at his feet therefore tied wings to his right ankle, which explains why Mercury is leaning to one side.

Two bronzes by Giovanni Francesco Susini also relate to Cupid. The casts of *Venus Burning Cupid's Arrows* and *Venus Chastising Cupid*, both of 1638, were likewise purchased by Prince Karl Eusebius. With his arrows, Cupid can direct the course of both human and divine love. After Cupid stirred up a liaison between his mother, Venus, and Mars, the god of war, Venus was not satisfied with merely burning his arrows. As a punishment, she tied her son to a myrtle tree and whipped him with rose branches, her left hand raised above her head in an instructive gesture.

Whereas the latter two bronzes have an obvious main viewpoint, the *Kneeling Woman Bathing* by the same artist is attractive from all sides. The complex serpentine body posture of the figure was borrowed by Susini from a work by Flemish-born Italian sculptor Giambologna, in whose Florentine studio Susini worked and who was a master of the *figura serpentinata* with its many angles of viewing. The author of the prince's inventory in 1658 described Susini's bronze as a 'small female figure cleaning and washing herself'.

An acquisition by Prince Johann Adam Andreas I was the bronze *Bacchus*. The lifesize figure is a copy of the famous sculpture of the wine god by the Renaissance artist Michelangelo, which was acquired by one of the Medici dukes. Massimiliano Soldani Benzi did a cast of it, though not to his client's

Giovanni Francesco Susini *c.* 1575–1653
Venus Chastising Cupid, 1638
Bronze with gold-brown patina, traces
of dark brown lacquer, height 58 cm
VIII.10

Giovanni Francesco Susini *c.* 1575–1653
Venus Burning Cupid's Arrows, 1638
Bronze with gold-brown patina, traces
of dark brown lacquer, height 56 cm
VIII.11

satisfaction. The elegant-looking Bacchus is shown here in company with a
painted satyr. Rubens depicted the hybrid creature from the god's retinue
with much less reserve.

Giovanni Francesco Susini *c.* 1575–1653
Kneeling Woman Bathing, 2nd quarter
of 17th century
after **Giambologna** 1529–1608
Bronze with gold-brown lacquer patina,
height 26 cm
VIII.9

GALLERY IX

17TH-CENTURY FLEMISH
AND DUTCH PORTRAIT PAINTING

After the triumph of Protestantism in northern Europe, altarpieces featuring Biblical subjects no longer formed the principal work for painters there. In consequence, portrait painting – hitherto a neglected genre – came into its own, and was taken up by better-known artists as well. In Protestant Holland, landscape and genre painting also flourished in the 17th century, with numerous artists specializing in the various painting genres. Because of the enormous output of the period, it is considered the golden age of Dutch painting.

PORTRAITS IN THE EARLY WORK OF PETER PAUL RUBENS

In Flanders, the Catholic part of the Netherlands, Peter Paul Rubens was the most sought-after painter of both religious subject matter and por-traits. The first major portrait com-missions, including the *Portrait of Jan Vermoelen*, came his way after he returned from Italy. In 1616, when Rubens painted him in three-quarter length, the young Antwerp-born sitter was on the threshold of a great career. Vermoelen is dressed ele-gantly in black. Framed by a white ruff, his face is modelled with lively colour highlights and set against a dark background, producing a strong sense of character. The sitter's alert

Peter Paul Rubens 1577–1640
Portrait of Jan Vermoelen, 1616
Oil on panel, 126 × 96 cm
IX.7

expression is directed out of the picture towards the right, while his body faces in the opposite direction. Despite the rigid conventions of portraiture, which allowed little freedom of composition or gesture in three-quarter-length portraits, Rubens managed to make a most interesting portrait. In the splen-did leather chair behind Vermoelen the ochre-coloured ground comes to the fore, a painterly effect that creates the illusion of leather.

In the case of portraits of his own children, which were intended to be kept by the family, the painter did not have to adhere to the traditional rules of portrait painting so closely. The *Portrait of Clara Serena Rubens*, dating from around 1616, shows the painter's daughter from his first marriage, to Isabella Brant, at the age of five. Leaning forward slightly, the girl looks the viewer

Peter Paul Rubens 1577–1640
Portrait of Clara Serena Rubens, c. 1616
Oil on canvas, mounted on panel,
37 × 27 cm
IX.1

directly in the eye. Her ruddy cheeks radiate a pulsating warmth that is
emphasized by highlights on her nose and forehead. The pale green of her
dress and the background form a neutral backdrop against which her face
and glossy, light-coloured hair stand out in contrast.

The double portrait of his sons Albert and Nikolaus Rubens, painted a decade
later, is not quite as candid as the portrait of Serena. Nine-year-old Nikolaus
takes no notice of the viewer, devoting his entire attention to playing with a
small goldfinch he holds tied to a line. Albert, meanwhile, who was four years
older at the time, seems scarcely a child any more. Elegantly dressed and
with grave mien, he looks out of the picture with his left arm round his young

Peter Paul Rubens 1577–1640
*Double Portrait of Albert and
Nikolaus Rubens, c.* 1626/27
Oil on panel, 157 × 93 cm
IX.2

Anthony van Dyck 1599–1641
Portrait of an Old Man, c. 1618
Oil on panel, 107 × 74 cm
IX.6

Anthony van Dyck 1599–1641
Portrait of a Genoese Nobleman, 1624
Oil on canvas, 131 × 101 cm
IX.3

brother. The book in his right hand draws attention to his scholarly achievements – at the time the portrait was made, he had just published his first poem in Latin.

EARLY PORTRAITS BY ANTHONY VAN DYCK

The impressive portraits from the early oeuvre of Anthony van Dyck are a major feature of the Princely Collections, and indeed constitute one of the largest accumulations anywhere. In Van Dyck's early pictures, the influence of Peter Paul Rubens is still readily apparent, since he worked as a master in Rubens's studio from 1618 to 1620/21. The coloration and the setting of the leather chair in the *Portrait of an Old Man* of around

Anthony van Dyck 1599–1641
Portrait of a Man, 1618
Oil on panel, 106 × 74 cm
IX.4

Anthony van Dyck 1599–1641
Portrait of a Woman, 1618
Oil on panel, 105 × 76 cm
IX.5

1618, for example, are reminiscent of those in the *Portrait of Jan Vermoelen* by Rubens. Like the latter, Van Dyck was constrained by the traditions of portrait painting in this three-quarters' profile, yet the individual, finely modelled facial features of the sitter have nevertheless been captured.

The twin paintings a *Portrait of a Man* and a *Portrait of a Woman* date from the same year. Both sitters are dressed in black and wearing white ruffs, which at the time had just come into fashion. Their stiffness further distances the sitters from the beholder. Despite the monochrome coloration, Van Dyck succeeded in lending the clothing a three-dimensional quality. Pairs of paintings of married couples like the ones in the Princely Collections were often commissioned on the occasion of a wedding, more to document the marital status than the couple's emotional attachment.

Around 1621, Van Dyck set off for Italy, where he remained for some years, to study the art of the Renaissance. This was also where he probably did the *Portrait of a Genoese Nobleman* of 1624. Genoa was a place that Van Dyck returned to many times, presumably taking advantage of contacts Rubens had made there. Thanks to the latter, the Genoese were already familiar with Flemish portraiture. In its warm, saturated colours running smoothly into each other, the portrait is clearly indebted to Venetian painting. The open body posture is also quite distinct from the sitters in Van Dyck's earlier por-

Anthony van Dyck 1599–1641
Portrait of Maria de Tassis, c. 1629/30
Oil on canvas, 128 × 92 cm
IX.12

Anthony van Dyck 1599–1641
Portrait of Antonio de Tassis, 1634
Oil on canvas, 126 × 89 cm
IX.8

traits. The gaze is directed out of the picture towards the right, while the nobleman's hands – likewise highlighted – point to the left.

By the time he returned to his native Antwerp, Van Dyck was much in vogue as a portraitist, his fame also having crossed the Channel to London, so that, at the invitation of Charles I, he spent the last decade of his life as a fêted court painter in England.

Before he left Flanders, he painted the *Portrait of Maria de Tassis* around 1629/30, a relation of the imperial postmaster in Antwerp. The three-quarters' portrait is one of the masterpieces of the Princely Collections. The young woman wears a silk dress trimmed with gold edging and lace. The exquisite material is masterly evoked and would seem to shimmer in the light. Despite the splendid dress and stately pose, the soft facial features of the sitter come across as natural and vivacious.

About four years later, Van Dyck painted another member of this family from Bergamo. The *Portrait of Antonio de Tassis* of 1634 shows Maria's father as a canon of Antwerp cathedral, an office conferred on him in 1630. The 50-year-old sitter looks at the viewer with a serious expression, the left side of his face remaining in shadow. He holds a book in his right hand as an indication of his scholarly interests – he was a noted art expert and left behind a major collection at his death.

Frans Hals 1580/85–1666
Portrait of a Man, 1650/52
Oil on canvas, 108 × 80 cm
IX.10

PORTRAITS BY FRANS HALS

Van Dyck's contemporary Frans Hals was the leading Dutch portraitist of the day. After the death of Rubens and Van Dyck, he even became the most sought-after portraitist in the Netherlands. In his *Portrait of a Man* of the early 1650s, there are no traces of the sitter's social status, and the sketchy grey background also provides no clues to the sitter's identity. Hals preferred to

Cabinet, Antwerp, shortly after 1650
Panel, tortoiseshell with red underlay,
bronze gilded, enamel, mirror-glass,
178 × 153 × 56 cm
IX.16

concentrate entirely on the facial features and hands of the man dressed in black, who looks roguishly at the viewer, the hint of laughter seeming almost mocking. His position somewhat to the left of centre reinforces the snapshot quality of the portrait. It was vividly unconventional portraits of this kind that brought Hals numerous commissions for portraits, both public and private.

Matthias Rauchmiller 1645–86
Resplendent tankard, 1676
Ivory, silver cup inside, height 35 cm
IX.21

APPLIED ART OF THE BAROQUE PERIOD

The richly decorated cabinet comes from Antwerp and is contemporary with
Hals's *Portrait of a Man*. It consists of an interior, the actual cabinet and the
table on witch it rests. The whole is articulated with architectural elements
such as columns and arches. The outside is inlaid with precious tortoiseshell.
The yellowish surfaces are underlaid with red, to create a strong overall
colour effect, and are mounted with gilt bronze ornamentation. When the
doors of the cabinet are open, another architectural arrangement in miniature
is visible inside, behind which a painted garden landscape gives the impression of spatial depth.

Giuliano di Piero Pandolfini doc.
1615–37
Pietra dura table-top, 1636
with the coat of arms of Prince Karl Eusebius von Liechtenstein
Comessi de pietre dure and gilt bronze,
129 × 94 cm
IX.14

The ornamental tankard is of ivory and was made by southern German crafts-man Matthias Rauchmiller in 1676. Prince Johann Adam Andreas I von Liech-tenstein acquired this masterpiece of Baroque ivory work at the beginning of the 18th century. The frieze round the body of the tankard depicts the Rape of the Sabine Women, with attackers and fleeing victims complexly interwov-en. The vehement movements of the figures in the round underscore the vio-lence of the episode from the early history of Rome. The delicately gleaming material that the craftsman used for both the handle and the lid form a sharp contrast to the body of the vessel.

It was Prince Karl Eusebius von Liechtenstein who bought the richly decorat-ed jasper tabletop, fashioned with the techniques of Florentine *pietra dura*

(cut polished stones inlaid in marble). Use was made of extremely expensive stones, such as the rich blue lapis lazuli, to produce the coloured flowers, animals and cartouches arranged symmetrically on the black marble top. Like the tabletop with the Liechtenstein armorial bearings (see p. 51), this table is from the workshop of Giuliano di Piero Pandolfini in Florence, which had established a name for its *pietra dura* work, in which mosaics were made with cut stone.

GALLERY X

Jan Brueghel the Elder 1568–1625
Landscape with the Young Tobias, 1598
Oil on copper, 36 × 55 cm
X.1

LANDSCAPE, STILL LIFE, GENRE PAINTING AND PORTRAITURE

In the 17th century, painting branched out in a number of new ways in the Netherlands. History painting with its mythological, religious or historical content remained the most highly regarded genre, but gradually individual aspects of it – landscape, still life and genre painting – became types in their own right. There were specialists for every genre, and they often undertook works without being commissioned to do so. This was because the client base itself had changed. After the Reformation, the Church commissioned rarely – it was burghers who had become rich and influential through commerce who formed the new elite and collected pictures. As a result of these changes, portrait painting also gained in popularity.

LANDSCAPE

Landscape had been popular as a backdrop for history scenes even in the Renaissance, and during the early 16th century it finally came into its own as an independent genre. However, paintings were done not in the open air, where at best mere sketches were made, but in the studio. Topographical accuracy was not the aim of such landscape pictures. Initially it was much more a case of fantasy landscapes composed on the basis of artistic criteria. Unlike most of his painter colleagues who had specialized in a particular field, Jan Brueghel the Elder was at home in many genres. The son of the famous Flemish landscape painter Pieter Brueghel the Elder, he was therefore much in demand, and worked for Rubens, among others. His *Landscape with the*

Gillis van Coninxloo 1544–1607
Forest Landscape, 1598
Oil on panel, 42 × 61 cm
X.3

Joos de Momper the Younger 1564–1635
Large Mountain Landscape, c. 1620
Figures presumably by **Hans Jordaens III**
c. 1595–1643
Oil on canvas, 226 × 327 cm
X.7

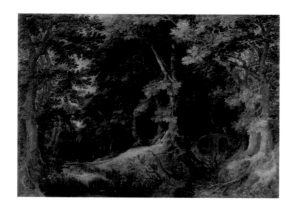

Young Tobias dating from 1598 is so densely populated with a colourful medley of figures that it is difficult to locate the Biblical scene it depicts. At the behest of the Archangel Raphael, Tobias has waded into the water on the left bank of the river in order to catch a fish whose gall bladder he can use to cure his father's blindness. The artist uses the technique of colour perspective to create an impression of spatial depth. The clearing in the wood in the left half of the picture is painted in tones of warm brown and green, while in the middle ground the colours are cooler and the distant mountains are bathed in a blue-grey haze.

Also a specialist in painting wooded landscapes was a contemporary of Jan Brueghel, Gillis van Coninxloo. His *Forest Landscape* in the Princely Collec-

Joos de Momper the Younger 1564–1635
Landscape with a Mountain Pass,
c. 1600 / 10
Oil on panel, 45 × 66 cm
X.2

tions, likewise from 1598, is a high point of Flemish landscape painting.
Quite unlike Brueghel, van Coninxloo was aiming at atmospheric effect in this
symmetrically arranged forest picture, employing strong contrasts of light
and dark. A traveller rests on an island in the middle of a densely forested
landscape while a group of figures crosses the stone bridge in the background.

Antwerp painter Joos de Momper the Younger was also a landscape specialist. Unlike van Coninxloo, it was mountain ranges that excited him, presumably as a result of his own experiences in the Alps. His *Large Mountain Landscape*, in which Momper assembled mighty rock formations, dates from
around 1620. The painter made use of strong light and shadow contrasts in
his works, thus reinforcing their fantastic character. He also often introduced
colour perspective into his pictures, as in the *Landscape with a Mountain
Pass* painted shortly after 1600. In both pictures, small staffage figures
convey a sense of the sheer size of the mountains.

Leiden-born painter Jan van Goyen specialized in depicting individual landscapes within Holland. He travelled extensively throughout the Dutch
provinces, recording his impressions in numerous sketches that later found
their way into his oil paintings done in the studio. His *The Rhine at Arnhem*
depicts the silhouette of the town beyond the river, which runs parallel to
the picture. The Groote Kerk in Arnhem, the symbol of the city, occupies the
largest part of the scene. In his works, van Goyen limited himself to a few
earthy tones, which blend together in easy transitions.

Jan van Goyen 1596–1656
The Rhine at Arnhem, 1645
Oil on panel, 65 × 97 cm
X.6

Philips Wouwerman 1619–68
Landscape with Bathers, c. 1660
Oil on canvas, 59 × 81 cm
X.8

Philips Wouwerman's *Landscape with Bathers* with its gentle hills and brick houses looks more Central European than Dutch. Several boys and men are seen bathing in a river in the pale sunlight of a spring day while two horsemen on the bank watch all the frolicking. The subject of 'landscape with

Willem van de Velde the Younger
1633–1707
Ships off the Coast, 1672
Oil on canvas, 45 × 55 cm
X.5

bathers' was often used as an excuse for idealized nudes. There is no trace of this in Wouwerman's painting – his figures are realistically depicted from life.

Seascapes were also popular with Dutch collectors in the 17th century. As the leading maritime country, Holland owed its success to the oceans. Willem van de Velde the Younger, the son of a marine draughtsman, specialized in this genre of painting. In pictures such as the *Ships off the Coast,* dating from 1672, he often included details from his father's drawings. Masts and sails rear up from various ships into a clouded sky. Just a few rays of the low-lying sun illuminate the clouds, creating a diffuse light.

Jan Davidsz. de Heem 1606–84
Fruit Still Life with a Silver Beaker, 1648
Oil on panel, 46 × 65 cm
X.28

Roelant Savery 1576–1639
Bouquet of Flowers, the so-called
Liechtenstein Bouquet, 1612
Oil on panel, 49 × 34 cm
X.30

STILL LIFE

In the 16th century, the still life led a shadowy existence. Of all painting genres, it ranked lowest because of the simple objects it featured. In the 17th
century, things changed as collectors began to develop a taste for the genre.
Here again specialists developed in the field for a variety of subjects, with
flowers and fruit still lifes enjoying the greatest popularity. Shooting and
fishing, with the associated gear, was another area where painters enjoyed
illustrating things down to the smallest detail, while other favourite subjects
included books and musical instruments. Because of their decorative effect,
monumental still lifes were just as popular in the 17th century as small,
delicately painted cabinet pictures for which collectors often paid large
sums.
One of the most skilled still-life painters of the period was Jan Davidsz. de
Heem, whose *Fruit Still Life with a Silver Beaker* of 1648 is one of the highlights of the Princely Collections. A green cloth is elegantly draped over a
wooden table, with various fruit, leaves and containers arranged on it. The
reflections of light on the silver and the brownish glass are rendered with
great precision, as are the drops of water on the individual grapes. De Heem
was a master in depicting material objects. The association of wine tendrils,
silver vessels and walnuts is known from Classical wedding customs, and
in this case could also be referring to the sacrament of marriage. A second
level of meaning of this kind underlay many 17th-century still lifes.

A secondary interpretation can also be assumed in the case of Roelant Savery's *Bouquet of Flowers* of 1612. In the small panel painting, the Flemish artist arranges flowers from the four seasons and phases of growth into a colourful bouquet. Likewise, the animals on the table allude to the four elements – the mouse stands for the earth, the bee for the air and the salamander for fire. The water in the vase completes the quartet. Cut flowers, as in *Bouquet of Flowers in a Niche*, represented the transience of earthly existence because of the brevity of their lives. The roughly symmetrically composed painting came from the brush of Ambrosius Bosschaert the Elder, one of the earliest Dutch specialists in flower still lifes. His flower arrangements are precise studies of nature and testify to the pleasure the artist derived from scientifically accurate renderings.

Ambrosius Bosschaert the Elder
1573–1621
Bouquet of Flowers in a Niche
Oil on panel, 35 × 23 cm
X.26

Jan van Huysum 1682–1749
Bouquet of Flowers
Oil on canvas, 89 × 71 cm
X.27

In the first half of the 18th century, Jan van Huysum was the leading still-life painter. His *Bouquet of Flowers* records flowers, leaves, fruit and animals with great accuracy. Pastel colour tones and a striving for decorative effect bear witness to the

Dionysio Miseroni *c.* 1607–61
Vase with cover (*Maienkrug*), 1639/40
with the coat of arms of the House of Liechtenstein and the Duchy of Troppau
Smoky quartz, gilt bronze, partly enamelled, 38 × 20 cm
X.35

stylistic trends of the Rococo period that spread throughout Europe in the early 18th century.

A still life in stone is what Dionysio Miseroni produced in 1639/40 for Prince Karl Eusebius von Liechtenstein. The Italian artist worked for a year on the six-side smoky quartz vase. Vessels of this kind were used to accommodate flower arrangements of agate. Precious stones were popular, highly regarded collector's items among art-loving princes. Ultimately, it was their rarity that made them eminently suitable as a distinguishing mark of princely rank.

Frans Snyders 1579–1657
The Lioness
Oil on canvas, 111 × 198 cm
X.23

Pieter de Bloot 1601–58
Christ in the House of Mary and Martha,
1637
Oil on panel, 47 × 66 cm
X.20

GENRE PAINTING

Genre painting likewise reached a high point in 17th-century Holland. A genre painting is one that shows the everyday life of various classes or occupational groups. The customs or mores depicted included aristocratic hunt scenes, peasant weddings or carousing in inns, and they are a rich source for modern social historians. But for contemporaries, as with still lifes, genre pictures often had a further layer of interpretation.

In the 16th century genre scenes were often combined with religious subject matter. In *Christ in the House of Mary and Martha* of 1637, Pieter de Bloot

Jan Miense Molenaer 1610–68
The King Drinks,
late 1630s
Oil on panel,
42 × 56 cm
X.21

Jan Steen 1626–79
The Fat Kitchen, late 1660s
Oil on panel, 36 × 45 cm
X.22

used the genre to show the contrast between faith and a life of pleasure. In the scene, Christ's encounter with the two women is more or less by the way. The focus in the foreground is a splendid kitchen still-life scene full of fruit, vegetables and other comestibles.

Jan Miense Molenaer's *The King Drinks* illustrates an Epiphany feast in Holland, where it was the custom for the Adoration of the Magi story to be acted out by amateur players like the ones in Molenaer's picture. Part of the cele-

Giovanni Francesco Susini *c.* 1575–1653
The Saccomazzone Players, 2nd quarter of 17th century
after **Orazio Mochi** (d. 1625) and **Romolo Ferrucci del Tadda** (d. 1621)
Bronze, golden-brown lacquer patina, height 42 cm (including socle)
X.36

Matthias Stom(er) *c.* 1600–after 1650
The Lutenist and the Flautist, 1640s
Oil on canvas, 90 × 79 cm
X.24

brations consisted of eating special cakes – the person whose cake had a bean in it was one of the three kings for the day. The painter shows an old woman getting the part – she is the one with a paper crown hanging on the back of her chair on the left edge of the picture. In the meantime, a young man trying to down a large tankard of beer is allocated the role of gluttony, one of the seven deadly sins.

The same subject is referred to in Jan Steen's *The Fat Kitchen.* A well-nourished family has assembled round a table in front of the fire. With a broad grin on his face, the master of the house cuts pieces off a large ham while the figure with its back to us in the foreground drains a glass. Painted in the late 1660s, the picture is

Matthias Stom(er) *c.* 1600–after 1650
The Adoration of the Shepherds, c. 1640/50
Oil on canvas, 117 × 166 cm
X.17

dominated by shades of brown, so that individual points of colour, such as the small girl's red cap, stand out.

Bronze caster Giovanni Francesco Susini's *The Saccomazzone Players* shows figures taking part in a popular peasant game. Using a stick like this, a blindfolded player attempts to hit another player. During the game, both players have to remain in contact with a stone placed in the middle of the play area. By choosing to use a very narrow base, Susini manages to intensify the wildness of the movements.

Along with eating, music-making in company was another favourite subject of genre painters. Matthias Stom(er)'s half-length figurative picture of musicians, *The Lutenist and the Flautist*, is full of extreme contrasts of light and dark. The warm candlelight illuminates the faces of the music-making figures, who stand out of the darkness like sculptures.

David Teniers the Younger 1610–90
Peasants Making Music, c. 1650
Oil on panel, 37 × 28 cm
X.19

Rembrandt Harmensz. van Rijn
1606–69
Cupid with the Soap Bubble, 1634
Oil on canvas, 75 × 93 cm
X.12

Gerrit Dou 1613–75
The Violin Player, 1653
Oil on canvas, 32 × 20 cm
X.25

Stom(er)'s preference for clearly modelled heads and hands is also evident in the large-format painting of *The Adoration of the Shepherds*. This was painted in Italy in the 1640s, where the Dutchman spent most of his active life. In the picture, the reddish reflection of light derives from the Christ Child, around whom the Virgin and the shepherds have gathered.

Joos van Craesbeeck's *The Lute Concert* of around 1650 is full of bright colours. Two women, one of them with her back turned to us, entertain a man by playing the lute to him. An elderly couple appear to be singing along as best they can, but even so the graceless gallant being serenaded is already asleep at the table. Diffuse light appears to emanate from the left, illuminating the white dress of the central figure.

Less crude is David Teniers the Younger's *Peasants Making Music* of around 1650. A trio consisting of a lutenist, wine-drinker and singer have gathered in a sitting room. But enjoyment of music appears to mean more to them than excessive wine drinking, since the carafe of wine is on the window sill and there is only a jug of water on the nearby table. Teniers's innocent depictions of peasant life made him one of the most popular painters of the 17th century.

The distinctive characteristic of his contemporary Gerrit Dou was a particularly precise technique, on account of which his style of small-scale work is

called *fijnschilderij* (fine painting). Dou's violin player of 1653 leans comfortably out of the window so as to watch what is going on in a nearby painter's studio, where a young man is grinding pigments to make paint. Dou's gift of meticulous observation shows in the sheet music ruffled by the wind and the richly adorned carpet.

An early work by Dou's teacher Rembrandt Harmensz van Rijn is also part of the Princely Collections. In his *Cupid with the Soap Bubble* of 1634, the god of love lies on a bed covered with a red cloth, making soap bubbles with a straw in a shell. The soap bubble serves here as a symbol of the transience of love, for whose capriciousness Cupid is partly responsible.

The bourgeoisie was also an object of genre scenes, as the *Portrait of a Young Woman* shows. The fashionable dress and white lace bonnet date the picture by Hendrik Gerritsz. Pot to the mid-1630s. The young girl sits at a table, her right hand lying on an open songbook. The small panel painting initially seems no different from other comedies of manners, as this kind of

Hendrik Gerritsz. Pot *c.* 1585–1657
Portrait of a Young Woman, c. 1635
Oil on panel, 44 × 34 cm
X.13

Eglon van der Neer 1634–1703
Young Woman at Breakfast, 1665
Oil on panel, 31 × 27 cm
X.11

genre painting is also known. But its companion piece, *Portrait of a Man*, indicates that it is in fact a portrait.

Similar in composition is the *Young Woman at Breakfast* of 1665 by Eglon van der Neer. The seated young woman in a fine red and white dress is placed prominently in the picture, while the arrangement on the table to the right of her (a wine glass, white stone jug, pewter plate with peeled lemon and oysters) looks like a still life in itself. In this late phase of genre painting, perfection of craft had priority over pictorial content, as is evident in the way van der Neer focuses on representing the different fabrics and objects.

PORTRAITURE

In the first half of the 17th century, there were three great portraitists at work in the Netherlands: Rubens, Rembrandt and Van Dyck. But the popularity of the genre is also evident in the portraits by their pupils and followers.

Samuel van Hoogstraten's *Self-portrait* dates from 1645, when the 18-year-old painter of this half-length portrait was still an apprentice in Rembrandt's studio. Soft light falls on the subject, casting a gleam on the golden chain he wears round his neck. Gold chains were an important

Pieter de Grebber *c.* 1600–52/53
Portrait of a Youth
Oil on panel, 79 × 62 cm
X.15

Samuel van Hoogstraten 1627–78
Self-portrait, 1645
Oil on panel, 54 × 45 cm
X.14

Godfried Schalcken 1643–1706
Self-portrait, 1679
Oil on copper, 43 × 32 cm
X.9

Godfried Schalcken 1643–1706
Portrait of Françoise van Diemen, 1679
Oil on copper, 43 × 32 cm
X.10

attribute of painting – gold indicated the high status of the genre, while the connected links symbolized the continuity of artistic tradition. In contrast, Pieter de Grebber's *Portrait of a Youth* looks almost theatrical in conception. It shows a young man showing off his high-rank clothes to the viewer.
Two small portraits in the Princely Collections are painted on copper – Godfried Schalcken's *Self-portrait* and the *Portrait of Françoise van Diemen*, the painter's wife. Schalcken was a pupil of two painters of the Rembrandt school, Samuel van Hoogstraten and Gerrit Dou. Perfect renderings in paint of various materials such as silk, brocade and lace were Schalcken's forte. The subjects are not only elegantly dressed but also shown surrounded by their works of art. Both have their right hand on their hearts, perhaps in reference to their marriage vows, which suggests the pictures were painted around 1679, the year the couple were married.

BIBLIOGRAPHY

Baumstark, Reinhold: *Meisterwerke der Sammlungen des Fürsten von Liechtenstein. Gemälde*, Zurich/Munich 1980.

Ausstellungskatalog *Peter Paul Rubens – Tod und Sieg des römischen Konsuls Decius Mus*, by Reinhold Baumstark, Staatliche Kunstsammlung Vaduz, Vaduz 1988.

Wagner, Harald: *Die Regierenden Fürsten von Liechtenstein*, Triesen 1995.

Schöpfer, Gerald: *Klar und fest. Geschichte des Hauses Liechtenstein*, Riegersburg 1996.

Wieczorek, Uwe (ed.)/issued by Kunststiftung der LGT Bank in Liechtenstein: *Meisterwerke der Sammlungen des Fürsten von Liechtenstein – Skulpturen, Kunsthandwerk, Waffen* (with texts by Maraike Bückling, Dirk Syndram, Johannes Ramharter), Berne 1996.

Lack, Hans Walter: *Ein Garten für die Ewigkeit – Der Codex Liechtenstein*, Berne 1999.

Liechtenstein Museum Vienna. Neoclassicism and Biedermaier, ed. Johann Kräftner, Munich/Berlin/London/New York 2004.

Liechtenstein Museum Vienna. The Collections, ed. Johann Kräftner, Munich/Berlin/London/New York 2004.

Liechtenstein Museum. A House for the Arts – the architecture of the Liechtenstein Museum in Vienna, ed. Johann Kräftner, Munich/Berlin/London/New York 2004.

INDEX OF ARTISTS

LIECHTENSTEIN MUSEUM.
The Princely Collections
Fürstengasse 1
1090 Vienna, Austria
Tel: +43 (1) 319 57 67-0
Fax: +43 (1) 319 57 67-20
E-Mail: office@liechtensteinmuseum.at
www.liechtensteinmuseum.at

OPENING TIMES
Daily except Tuesdays: 9 am–8 pm
The garden can be visited during
museum opening hours.

VISITOR SERVICES, INFORMATION,
REQUESTS FOR GUIDED TOURS
Tel: +43 (1) 319 57 67-252
Fax: +43 (1) 319 57 67-255
E-mail: info@liechtensteinmuseum.at
Infopoint in the museum

MUSEUM SHOP
Opening hours:
as for the museum
Web shop:
http://shop.liechtensteinmuseum.at

RESTAURANT, BAR, CAFÉ
Rubens's Brasserie
Opening times:
daily except Tuesdays, 9 am–midnight
Reservations: +43 (1) 319 23 96-11
Fax: +43 (1) 319 23 96-96
Rubens's Palais
Opening times: Tuesday–Saturday,
noon–5 pm and 6:30 pm–midnight
Reservations: +43 (1) 319 23 96-13
Fax: +43 (1) 319 23 96-96
www.rubens.at
Garden for guests in the *cours
d'honneur*

GETTING THERE
Tram
Line D to Seegasse or Bauernfeld-
platz stops
Lines 37/38/40/41/42 to Sensen-
gasse, then on foot to Strudlhofstiege
and the Fürstengasse entrance
Underground railway (U-Bahn)
U2: Schottentor station, then bus
route 40A to Bauernfeldplatz
U4: Rossauer Lände station, then
about 600 m on foot to the Fürsten-
gasse entrance
U4: Friedensbrücke station,
then 300 m on foot to the park
entrance
Bus
Route 40A to Bauernfeldplatz
Bus stops Fürstengasse/
corner of Liechtensteinstrasse